Uncurling Freedom

Lorna Westergreen

Uncurling Freedom

Copyright ©2018 Jennifer Maxwell

Cover designed by Rick Magley, Universal Images Design Lab

All rights reserved.

ISBN-13: 978-1729517970
ISBN-10: 1729517978

Scripture quotations marked KJV are taken from the *Holy Bible*, King James Version. This authorized version was commissioned by King James I of England in 1604, completed and published in 1611, and is now in the public domain.

Scripture quotations marked JBP are taken from *J.B. Phillips Translation*, copyright © 1960, 1972 J.B. Phillips. Administered by the Archbishops' Council of the Church of England.

No part of this publication may be reproduced, stored in a retrieval system, or transmitted in any form or by any means — electronic, mechanical, photocopy, recording, or any other — except for brief quotations in printed reviews, without the prior permission of the author.

Printed in the United States of America

Uncurling Freedom

Uncurling Freedom

Dedication

To My Brother — Claude Louis — Beautiful boy —
(beau garcon) Fr.

My heart and life are spread out all over these pages.

Uncurling Freedom

TABLE OF CONTENTS

7   Miracle Offspring

27   African Adventures

53   South Sudan

87   A Tribute to Claude Louis

101 Where is Home?

105 Journey of Faith

115 Vigilant Protection

121 Emotional Color

125 Heart Trauma

129 What's My Story?

135 Remembering Mum

141 Biblical Mandate

145 Duplicitous Character

153 Change: Mabadiliko (Kiswahili)

159 Uncurled Freedom

Uncurling Freedom

Uncurling Freedom

MIRACLE OFFSPRING

What color would my children be when they presented their little selves to the formidable world?
Looking back into my own childhood and the lineage of my dad and mum, I struggled with the question.

Mum's parents were from Sweden and France, called the "Great Whites." Dad's parents were from England, Ireland and Scotland — the average Seychellois.

The Seychelles Islands were made up of people from all over the world, including Africa. Intermarriage was common, and many remarkable and exceptional people of color were born. These islands were made up

Uncurling Freedom

of a kaleidoscope of azure oceans and various people. Color undeniably was the most flamboyant feature.

As I grew up in Kenya under the British regime, so much racial bias was directed at those of us whose parents came from the exotic islands. Anyone not born "pure white" from Europe or the British Isles was considered half-caste.

This term was a yoke of oppression dominating and tarnishing our lives. The colonizers were not even able to mention those islands. They simply said, "They are from there."

I had no clue I was untouchable and did not meet the "color" bar. After my salvation in 1957, I attended a church where to my alarm this same prejudice portrayed its ugly face. Not only did the colonial community profile me, but also the missionary community. I carried this excess baggage with me when I went to Bible School in New York.

Paul and Gloria, missionary pastors of the church I attended in Nairobi, were the only people who treated me well. Many years later they wrote to me, "In 1962, in Nairobi we only saw a beautiful young woman

Uncurling Freedom

with so much potential. We were and are so proud to include you in our family. My mom and dad never had anything bad to say about you. They loved you because of you."

Imagine being loved because of who I am and not for my color!

It took me many decades to see that I am not measured by my past, my pedigree or my color but by my potential. This truth is what God, Paul and Gloria saw when they reached into my life in Kenya. They saved me from a possible life of drugs and prostitution which was the expectation for half-caste women.

When I arrived at Bible school students met me with nonverbal questions. Or they mentioned things such as, "You have blue eyes. How come?" They added to my baggage with the question of my color and acceptance in the white community.

After Bible school and marriage to Zack, we moved to Staten Island, New York, where we assisted Pastor James in the youth ministry. We all fondly called him, PT. He had the vision, and we made it work. We worked in the projects and on the streets in the summer,

Uncurling Freedom

started outdoor mid-week summer praise and worship meetings under the stars. An influx of young people from the projects came to Christ.

This experience was such an amazing, challenging, stretching and validating time under the tutelage of Pastor James. We flourished. The church members embraced us when they witnessed the reality of Pastor James's vision for the youth. Life could not have been better.

Then I got pregnant. Endless months passed as I fretted, stewed and grieved about what this child's color would be. I was so distressed. Pastor James, being the insightful and caring godly man he was, walked with me through those dark and formidable months.

Then the day arrived when the birth of my first child was imminent. We attended special evangelistic meetings and I was part of the choir.

Suddenly I realized I needed to get to the hospital, and I went into a tailspin. What if my child was born black?

I had an excellent Roman Catholic gynecologist whose tender care helped me through the trauma of my

Uncurling Freedom

first child's birth. I almost died with pre-eclampsia. I went into convulsions and the baby was almost crushed to death.

Philo was born tow-headed with sparkling blue eyes. His brother Elior followed 13 months later with brown doe eyes and brown hair. Both were white! Five years later, in Kenya, a little sister joined them with brown-green eyes and beautiful brown hair.

Before Diani's birth, we were attending All Nations Gospel church and sat next to an African lady. Elior watched as she made preparations to breastfeed her baby. She reached down into her turtleneck sweater, produced an elongated breast and promptly stuck it into the hungry infant's gaping mouth.

Elior watched all this at eye level. Then he turned to me, jabbed his elbow to my bulging belly and asked, "Will you do that Mum?"

"Yes."

Those beautiful long lashed eyelids, brown doe eyes and mouth together said, "Oh!"

This moment was the first miraculous gift from God to me. All my preconceptions and baggage handed

Uncurling Freedom

over to me from my childhood in Kenya simply flew out the window.

There is nothing wrong with black children or being a black person. The hardest part of this story is the prejudgment, prejudice, assumption and expectations. Yokes placed on my shoulders by insecure people injured my life, self-worth and value.

The siblings in my family and many others were not able to jump over such hurdles. They limped through life. Graciously, God brought Pastor James across my painful emotional trek. He and his wife were able to "gentle" me through those years in New York.

Our first African assignment was to be Kinshasa, Congo. Being from a French background, I had little problem with French, but Zack had to buckle down and learn the language. We were very thankful when our mission reassigned us to Kenya—my homeland, in September 1972. We settled into the routine and ministry in Nairobi with some good and happy days. The boys started nursery school, and each day Zack took them on his motorbike.

Uncurling Freedom

My little children were very tired when they came home from school, but Zack forced them to eat lunch. After naps, when failing to reach the toilet in time, Zack tipped Elior upside down and wiped his nose in his urine. Tender little emotions were stuffed and buried deep down. This abusive scenario caused steel and hardness to develop in Elior.

It became evident in 1974 when Diani was born that a serious problem had taken root in our marriage.

On one occasion, Zack drove fast down the highway to see a safari rally in Nairobi. When I became frightened by the speed he was driving, I voiced my fear. Somehow or other, my fear blinded Zack with anger. His rage erupted. He pulled off the road and forced my baby and me to get out of the vehicle. He drove away with Philo and Elior. I was left standing alone on the highway. I had to walk many kilometers home. This incident impacted my five- and six-year-old children as a scarring of their little souls began.

I had no house key so waited outside until Zack's return. Thankfully, I was breastfeeding the baby.

Uncurling Freedom

Upon Zack's return there was no discussion about this appalling treatment.

A door had opened, a crossroad reached. Which way would I go?

I had no recourse. In order to continue on the field, I developed a hiding and silence mentality. Because his abuses were not addressed, the perpetrator took liberty and delight in his mistreatment of us. For the next 46 years, he emotionally, mentally and verbally violated not only me, but also my children and then my grandchildren.

The years rolled by. My children grew up and the miracle continued. They developed resilience at early ages. They tried to put back the broken bits, to seek wholeness, purpose and a future, as they became members of a community.

These were small steps of renovation, but bands of pain gripped our hearts. The parent, who was meant to care for and cherish each child, was literally scarring them in soul and body.

"The idea that we cannot be abusing of children if we are not hitting them could not be farther from the

Uncurling Freedom

truth. Emotional abuse traumatizes a child just as swiftly. It is unforgiving, relentless and quiet in its path. It slowly destroys children by stripping them of their self-esteem, emotions, trust and more. Each child is affected differently but they are affected." - Elisabeth Kubler-Ross

Had I understood what was going on, I would have stepped in. My negligence and inaction cost us all a great deal. I may have done more to protect these little innocents from his brutality, but I was crushed into submission. I actually gave into him, lost my voice and so much of who I was. To this day I still search for the real me.

For many years, I have carried my pain around and taken on the suffering of my children. No matter how hard Zack tried to extinguish me with his rage, anger and violence, the less he succeeded, the more rage developed.

I was unshakable. I never gave up.

A seed of redemption was planted in me in Kenya. I watched it germinate and take root in my children. The miracle continued.

Uncurling Freedom

Diani wrote: "None of us kids would be what we are today without the sacrifice you made, Ma. It was because of God's love and grace through you, Mum, that we were NOT more drastically affected. The choices you made cannot be second-guessed. You never stopped seeking God's face, wisdom and strength through it all. You have demonstrated to all of us what it truly means to be faithful. You are still doing this. I am sorry you sacrificed so much of who you are and wanted to be, but every day you are still fighting to stay alive mentally, physically and spiritually with God's strength, for his glory. You continue to inspire and be JESUS to those all around you. Satan wants you to get bogged down in history. Don't put your focus there. Continue to live and love and keep your eyes on the PRIZE. One day you will laughing and dancing and whole."

In 1976, we located to Karamaini Estate, Bob Harries's Farm in Thika. Our landlord, a White Kenyan believer, offered us a delightful thatched-roof house in the middle of a coffee and bird of paradise plantation. We called it, "The Farm."

Uncurling Freedom

Avocado trees surrounded the house. Cows strolled just over the fence and provided our milk. A dam provided the perfect place for catching fish and playing. A small airstrip with apple mango trees dotted the runway.

Huge pythons came up from the river to challenge our dogs. Giant forest hogs attacked our dogs and us at night. We lived a story similar to the movie, "Out of Africa." Dullness was never part of our lives.

The children attended Imani school (British curriculum) located in the middle of a huge Del Monte pineapple plantation. During the rainy season, getting there posed real hazards. The car would slip off the muddy road with a load of school children. Truckloads of happy coffee pickers manually lifted us out of the ditch and back onto the road.

When Diani was two years old, she would line up our pedigree German shepherd dogs outside the kitchen, open up her Bible and make them listen to her sermons. When I could not find her, I would walk up to Mama Elizabeth's house and find them sitting by

Uncurling Freedom

an open fire. Each talked in her own language, ate collard greens and cornmeal.

Once a year, Philo and Elior entered contests for baking cakes at the Nairobi show. They won many awards. They trained their own pedigree German shepherd dogs and ran them in the Nairobi Dog show. Such hilarity was created as I drove our Peugeot station wagon, towing Zack on his damaged motorbike. The two boys shouted and waved their arms out the windows to warn cars, people and motorbikes not to come between us.

We camped in tents at Lake Naivisha with Canadian and Australian Salvation Army missionaries. During the night, we would not dare go to the loo. Outside the tents, we might encounter marauding hippos, crocodiles and flamingos.

One school holiday, we set out on a secret expedition from "The Farm" to Nairobi Train Station. Our destination was Mombasa, which dipped into the India Ocean. Glittering white sandy beaches and coconut palms with monkeys swinging through them were all along the shoreline. We saw beautiful African

Uncurling Freedom

people walking along the white sands selling fish and colorful fabrics, sharing their Africa with us. A song from my own youth about the land of Kenya encapsulated that train ride. Clinking, clanging, belching smoke, stopping and starting on its12-hour ride to the Indian Ocean (The East African Railways and Harbors).

Our compartment had two bunk beds. The Railway staff, dressed in white Kanzu (The Arab floor-length garment worn by East African men), came to make up the beds. They delivered steaming cups of hot Kenya Chai tea. We breakfasted in the "restaurant car" with lovely white tablecloths, huge silver forks, knives and spoons, again piping hot Kenyan tea, and a full British breakfast. As we chugged along the railway line, outside was this breath-taking vista dotted with wild animals, herds of cattle and villages. With a medley of such beauty, we were spell-bound. Creation at its best.

Arriving in Mombasa, we found a taxi to the ferry that took us across the harbor filled with man-eating sharks. Back on the mainland, we walked up to

Uncurling Freedom

the CPK guesthouse, lugging our cases. We enjoyed a pool, sundowners at sunset, mangos and lovely meals. Diani learned to swim at that pool when she was three years old. At five years old, she became a champion swimmer in Kenya.

It was in this idyllic life and setting that the physical abuse increased. A seething hot and erupting pool that could bubble over in a moment's notice and ruin a perfect holiday. In the midst of all this adventure, challenge, excitement and fear — things most people only see in movies — an underlying terror stalked each of us.

Any infractions by the boys meant being bent over the bed and beaten with a leather belt. Then they were forced to hug and pray for forgiveness with their father. False acts of love.

The undercurrent of forced brutality added to demands that things must be done Zack's way. Otherwise he would erupt, and a lovely journey would turn into a nightmare.

The face Zack showed to the outside world was such a contrast. The Charmer. He was overseer of 40

Uncurling Freedom

churches, the mission's area representative, building churches with multiple speaking and teaching engagements.

The background of all this pain and torment placed steel into the hearts of my children.

After years of struggling academically in primary school, Philo attended a missionary boarding school. With the help of godly teachers, he graduated. They set an example for the type of person he wanted to be.

He did his basic training in the Army. He grew into a man and learned how to live in the USA after growing up in Africa. He was able to do his Advanced Individual Training in the army as a Medic, with a Presidential Citation as an outstanding soldier. He then attended University, graduating as a teacher.

Tanzania had a need for a teacher in a one-room schoolhouse. Philo applied and was assigned to that post. His pre-field orientation counselor picked up on his hidden angers and addressed them. Philo's comment to the counselor was, "I do not want to be like my father."

Uncurling Freedom

Thankfully the counselor helped him. Philo continued to grow into the type of person he wanted to become. He later obtained his Administrator's degree and served in Kenya, Rwanda and the Philippines in this capacity.

Elior had an easier time educationally, but was deeply affected and traumatized by his father. He ploughed through school and worked his way through University obtaining his Bachelors and Masters in Construction Management.

This child still has such buried pain. He is a man of honor and integrity and excels at his work, but inside he is crumbling into pieces. He will not allow anyone into his inner sanctum.

Diani was the strong child. She would not allow her father to treat her as he did the rest of us. She spoke up to him and it cost her. She graduated from University in Occupational Therapy and grew strong as a godly wife and mother.

God's grace continued to extend to my children as we served in Kenya. Along with such grace was also God's provision—mysterious, but always there.

Uncurling Freedom

How did God do this? He did it because He saw in me availability and purpose in service.

God continues to restore what was destroyed, broken and snuffed out in the work he does in us today. It filters into my children and their children, flowering into productive growth.

When Diani crawled out of bed each morning, she knelt to pray. When I asked her why this was her practice, she said, "This is what I saw you do, Mama."

My children have not been cast aside, but remain running the race of life. This is a lasting miracle.

As Cecil Murphy writes, "Secrets trapped us in the past. Now we're free to live without secrets in the present."

Philo sent a letter on May 24 1994: "Mum and Dad, here I sit writing with my new Parker fountain pen, a gift of which I am most grateful. One of my students got it for me, and it brings back many memories of Thika, and Imani school days.

"In fact, the other day I was getting a cold, so I cut up a couple of oranges and thought of that little green trailer, orange mesh plastic bags, East African

Uncurling Freedom

Bag and Cordage and of course Juja town. As we all know they were the best, but still cannot compare to the good times we had.

"Life was good to us, was it not? I still do not think I could have had a better childhood, thanks to both of you. For days at the dam, windsurfing at children's holiday in Mombasa, orange slices in our lunch with the top parts cut off, gumboots in the rain, puppies, killer pigs, motorcycles, rugby games at Kenton College, hockey matches, winning parent duos in the 50 metre sprint, camping at Safari Park...top of the escarpment, cutting Christmas trees on the way home through the forest, lunch at the club, airport farewells, Mike Hall, Bill Herlin, Ernie Gruin, best goodies at RVA, finishing off projects in the woodshop, Mombasa, Naivasha, pellet guns, monkeys in the garden, big snakes, hot water tank, meringue with cream and strawberries, walking to get milk, tract storage facilities on fire, Charles, Margaret, Jerome, Patrick, Chell Chell (le petit chien, dog), 7 system TV and VCR, drive-in movies, Longonot volcano, sanding benches at church, trees, trees, trees, bougainvillea,

Uncurling Freedom

lunch at the club, a new sister, Lindsays, Riches, McKeands, Louts, area meeting, Aunty Prinsic, Manor lunches, extra free weekends, big hugs, apartment at John Brown University, great food and love.

"Heavens Paros (Kenya Sheng for parents), I've had so much and I thank the Lord for you are the best. As I am, you probably get a little teary too, but it makes us who we are today. I just want you to know, that I know, that you gave us your all. Thanks, Philo."

Tears are like melting snow flakes, touching God's heart and moving him to share our sorrow. I want to live a life of no regrets.

Uncurling Freedom

Uncurling Freedom

AFRICAN ADVENTURES

Re-Entry:

Going to Africa was far simpler to live, adjust and assimilate into the culture. Perhaps because Africans are kind. "Wema hauozi" kindness is never wasted.

The same was not true upon our return to the first world.

Like a cyclone whirling inside me, I was unable to keep up to the speed of life in the United States.
Before I finished dialing a phone number, it was ringing. In Africa, I dialed numbers and waited several minutes listening through all the clicks and chucks before it went through. In Africa, there is real time.

Uncurling Freedom

I did not fit in and wasn't sure I wanted to become like "them." A people with blinders on their eyes, they seemed to see only the immediate picture of life — not the broader worldview which colored and challenged me to be and do so much more.

I bought real potatoes in Africa, but so much food in the USA was artificial or automatic with endless shelves to choose from.

Was I worth loving and belonging? If so — where?

Brene Brown writes, "If I want to fully experience love and belonging, I must believe that I am worthy of love and belonging. True belonging doesn't require that we change who we are; it requires that we be who we are."

My self-esteem was at rock bottom. How could I be who I really am? I lay on the ground and wondered how I could possibly continue. My children were silent, not knowing what words to use or how to fit in.

When someone asked me, "How are you doing, Lorna?" and I began to answer, they had no patience to

Uncurling Freedom

really listen. In reality they did not want to know about my transition or the complicated erupting emotions, the struggling with feelings that constantly abused me.

It was almost as if I was two people, and only one person thrived in Africa. Was there a glimpse of hope where my feet landed, a spark of something to accept how I lived in Africa and how I now had to live in America?

My whole being — body, soul, spirit felt torn between two continents.

A beautiful African entered the American winter. Perhaps twigs of green would shoot out from my life if spring were to come. Absolutely nothing worked. I felt dislocated and frustrated. I was not able to get back in step.

Would anyone walk alongside me and explain all this, approaching life cold turkey? A deep and dark depression descended. I felt as if I was in solitary confinement.

God seemed to whisper, *Choose not to get depressed. Walk every day. Take up your bed and dance.*

Uncurling Freedom

Dancing with no African music or people was illusive.

Survival. God took my hand. His strength helped me get out of bed, walk and dance, in the very confusing and blessed land of America.

Few Americans honored me for my service in Africa, for being compassionate to people of a different color than I. The Africans were his real treasures hidden in the dark where no one could see them.

I lived a life most people would be afraid to choose. I met insurmountable challenges and became stronger emotionally—a more compassionate person, helping the needy even while I was so barren inside.

Did helping the needy African quench my own hunger for love and belonging? No. Love should have come from the husband of my youth. But such loss did not deter me. Somehow reaching and satisfying such hunger in my African family, gave me a glimpse of hope to keep going.

I no longer heard the African thunder nor smelled the rain when it first splattered on our parched and hungry land. Nor did I see the flying ants around

Uncurling Freedom

light poles or hear squealing African children collecting the ants in buckets for their breakfast.

Tentatively, I saw Jesus's excitement and pleasure when he looked at me, encouraging me to continue the race in this different land.

Who else was there to join the cheering?

Household Tasks:

Working on a building project in Kitui, we needed input. Housing teams from the USA could help us. I had never facilitated large groups before and it frustrated me as to how I could possibly manage. Especially since we lived three hours away from good food supplies.

Our friends were bringing in teams to build the Nazarene University in Nairobi, and Row shared all the logistics. "Bring in a team of 10 people. The team will donate X amount of dollars to the project and their upkeep and work for two weeks." Row also gave me recipes for feeding the "5000." They worked, but all the supplies had to be brought in from Nairobi in advance.

Uncurling Freedom

Our Indian Muslim neighbor allowed me to transfer all our meat and cold cuts to his deep freezer. Fresh produce was laid out on the cold laundry room floor, covered with wet sheets. I enlisted two team members as the food crew, because we had to make everything from scratch. I served two meals at our house and made lunch to take to the building site.

We housed all ten people on bunk beds, but had specific instructions not to use the inside toilet. They had to use the "long drop" or "pit latrine" outside. Square holes were dug, and then trees or planks put over the top, with a hole cut in the middle. A small house was then built over the top. To use, they squatted over the hole, took aim, and relieved themselves.

My first time doing this; I was unprepared for crickets coming out of the sewer pit, aimed right at my buttocks. It shook me up so much I ran out of the building without pulling up my undergarments. The next time before squatting, I banged on the wooden floor and the sides of the building. I wanted to make sure a snake was not hiding inside.

Uncurling Freedom

Showers were minimal, and water was collected out of the bathtub for the toilet.

The team fondly called me "Major" as precision and tactical logistics were my domain. After full days of work, dinner and showers, the team went back to the church for teaching and ministry. On Sundays, they traveled to the villages. I had to send packed lunches with them, as we did not want them getting sick from eating local food.

Before returning to the USA, we took them on a two-day safari. They left fulfilled, satisfied, with the accomplishment of good work.

I employed some African ladies, who came early every day to do laundry by hand on our postage stamp-sized front lawn. It was amusing to see these ladies squat on the ground beside large containers of soapy water. Then into the clean water and the laundry wrung out by hand. Water trucks came daily to replenish the supply. Lines were strung up from our windows to the fence to dry all the clothes. Navigating the clothes lines from the house to the gate was hilarious.

Uncurling Freedom

As all this was going on, we had endless electricity problems. The landline would suddenly decide to quit right in the middle of a word.

At the end of each day, I fell into bed, beaten into exhaustion. I literally picked up one foot and put it down, then picked up the next foot. Could this exhaustion cause me to really listen to God's voice?

Saint John of the Cross "Encourages us not to give up because in this stage of my relationship the hard work of love really begins." - Adam McHugh.

I know this activity helped the project and God's work in Africa, but it did little to build my self-esteem. Perhaps I was serving to stifle my own pain and the loss of a meaningful married life. Perhaps I did everything to hide my own need.

In the middle of this whirl of challenges, I was vitally connected to my Sustainer.

As I cared for the team, I also cared for pastors and their families. Making up packages of rice, beans, sugar, maize, and tea — especially in times of severe famine in our area. Perhaps my addiction to help needy African children was a life-saving salve.

Uncurling Freedom

On the team's journey out, comments were made that they had never seen a couple work together so well. We were experts in hiding the painful truth about the real life we lacked.

Alone with Health Risks:

In March 2014, I noticed small amounts of blood in my urine. I frowned a bit and left it at that. By October, I experienced a major bleed-out for 24 hours. Every time I urinated, clots and chunks of blood poured out. I was not afraid or angry. It was just one more thing God was allowing me to walk through, and I knew the power belonged to him to work out the details. Of course he gave me a level head, hands and feet on the ground to bring about some form of solution.

I kept quiet and did not tell Zack, given his self-attention, absorption and work focus for the Foundation. It was something I needed to do myself. Why would I ask for his help when throughout our whole life his hand of support was elsewhere?

I had to manage myself, so I did.

Uncurling Freedom

God's words to me were from Deuteronomy 33:25, *"The bolts of your gates will be iron and bronze, and your strength will equal your days"* (KJV).

With everything I had experienced, I asked God, "Why is so much required of me?"

He held me to his Word. For each day there would be sufficient strength.

I emailed a urologist at Tenwek Mission Hospital in Kenya. He sent a prescription with an urgency to get my urine tested. The Foundation we volunteered with in Kigali would not allow volunteers to use their vehicles, so I had to walk and ride busses to the King Faisal Hospital. I donated my urine for testing.

When I arrived at the hospital lab for my results, the technician refused to give them to me. "You must speak with the radiologist," he said.

He eventually came out of the lab, grim-faced and told me I had bladder cancer. I did not shout, scream or throw a fit, but simply accepted the fact for what it was.

Uncurling Freedom

I have cancer. Sickness and physical ailments have never been a public thing with me. I hold these things close. Few people even know I am ill.

The director of the foundation where we volunteered in Rwanda took offence that I would not share my diagnosis with him. Another man addicted to himself, in the name of God, of course.

I would not even ask for help with transport getting to the hospital, because the director would burrow into my personal life.

As there were no credible urologists in Rwanda, the American missionary urologist at Tenwek asked, "Will you travel to Kenya for a cystoscopy and surgical removal of cancer should that be needed?"

The journey took an entire day as we flew out of Kigali to Nairobi, rode a taxi from the airport to Tenwek Mission hospital, a six-hour drive away, and settled into the mission guesthouse. Our reason for choosing this option was the expense. We were no longer able to afford medical insurance. Tenwek offered qualified medical care at minimum cost provided by missionary doctors from all over the world.

Uncurling Freedom

For the first surgical procedure, I had a spinal. Specimens had to be sent to Aga Khan Hospital in Nairobi for determination. One procedure needed cauterization, as the cancer was so small. The urologist asked if I could manage without painkillers and I agreed. He was amazed that I was able to lie there and take the pain, even talking as he removed the cancer. All recurring bladder cancer was high-grade non-muscle invasive TCC.

While at Tenwek, I met a urologist from Indiana who gave his vacation time to help people like the African community and me. If I could travel to Indiana, he would treat me pro bono with Bacillus Calmette-Guerin for six weeks. This treatment was the main intravesical immunotherapy for early-stage bladder cancer.

Dear friends in Indiana hosted me for the six weeks of treatment. Our car was in storage near them, so I was able to learn to drive again. For the first two sessions, one of our friends drove me three hours to Avon, Indiana. My daughter–in–law gave up her spring break to help me for two weeks. During the last two

Uncurling Freedom

weeks I completed the six-hour round trip and treatment alone. The treatment had very few side effects. Hopefully I have five "grace" years.

As I went through this process, urologists at Tenwek explained how I contracted bladder cancer. With our 12 years of bush work in Kitui, wading and helping push disabled vehicles through rivers contaminated by defecating people and animals, I became infected with Schistosomiasis. All it takes is one snail, a worm and some fresh water to become infected. In parts of Africa, schistosomiasis is a widespread problem. The disease can persist for decades and can prove fatal.

Having bladder cancer brought no concern to me, nor does it in the present. I have lived a long and amazing life with gifted children and grandchildren, many African friends and their children. I have travelled the world, lived through tribulation, dark valleys and blistering deserts. I have been shamed and humiliated, verbally tormented.

But I have also experienced ecstasy at the birth of six of my eight grand girls, rafted down rapids on the

Uncurling Freedom

Nile river, visited my mother lands of France and Norway. By God's grace, I have navigated most of life's storms.

For a person who came from the wrong side of the tracks, life could not have been better. Beyond expectations. I have kept my eyes on Jesus, waiting to see him face to face and hear him say, "Well done, good and faithful servant."

He holds my redeemed and broken heart in his tender and careful hands. He keeps his strong hand on my shoulder, urging me forward—up and over all obstacles.

"I press toward the mark for the prize of the high calling of God in Christ Jesus" (Philippians 3:14 KJV).

The only loss was that of a mate who would cherish and care for me. I grieve for such loss and loneliness, for the emptiness that is unutterable.

It has been asked of me, "Lorna, you have helped so many others, why could you not help yourself?"

What I could not do, Jesus did for me.

Letting Philo Go to the Kuwait War:

In January, 1991, we received a phone call from Philo. He was reactivating his status in the US Army Reserves as a combat medic, and would proceed to Kuwait and the Gulf War. We were miles away from him, in the Kenyan bush. We could not even reach out a hand to pray for his decision.

This news shattered my heart into millions of pieces. At his birth, God gave me this verse for him from First Samuel 1:28, *"Therefore also I have lent him to the LORD; as long as he lives he shall be lent to the LORD"* (KJV).

As I had lent him to God, I could not take back a promise. I knew God would care for his life wherever Philo would go. Before his documentation came through, the war ended.

In 1997, Philo and his wife worked at the American International School, Kuwait City, Kuwait, as teachers. Their first child, Zed, was born there in 1999.

Uncurling Freedom

Terrorist Bombing in Nairobi:

The United States Embassy was bombed in Nairobi, August 1998. Philo and his wife had come from Kuwait to assist us for three weeks with the Kitui Church Project. The whole city shook. Philo and his wife were in a skyscraper organizing tickets back to Kuwait. They felt the building sway and heard the boom.

We were all in different locations of the city and had no way to communicate. In those days mobile phones were non-existent. Finally we all ended up at our Nairobi apartment. What a relief that none of us was injured! The city was awry with people running, driving and hurrying out of the city center. Those we passed in the streets were soaked in blood.

Philo and I decided to go Kenyatta National Hospital and help with the wounded and dying. As he is a qualified army medic, the team of doctors and nurses welcomed him. The Hindu, Muslim, Indian and European communities, along with all Rotary clubs and the general public flooded the hospital with medical

Uncurling Freedom

supplies. We spent hours suturing, binding, cleaning and saving lives. People were strewn on the floors all over the hospital.

My son and I were shaken, taking care of the wounded and dying. As we cared for them prayer barely escaped our lips, so traumatizing was the experience. We personally gave thanks that we were spared bodily harm. We prayed for those who knew not the King of Kings. Evil presented itself in my country, but that evil did not encroach on my soul.

I felt stronger helping other people. Perhaps Jesus designed life for me to reach out, uplift and change the lives of the destitute and needy. I understand what they are going through. I have walked that path ever since I can remember.

Kitui — Home Alone:

As resident missionary, Zack assisted in overseeing 40 churches in the district. I never knew where he was until he reached a town with one phone. He called any time of the day or night to let me know he was okay. To reach the churches he drove through

Uncurling Freedom

overflowing rivers, vast desert areas, possible encounters with armed Shifta bandits and wild animal poachers. Added to this were the overloaded busses and small vans hurtling along dangerous roads, many involved in major accidents. 50 dead at one time was a common occurrence.

In Kitui, we sometimes pushed disabled vehicles through rivers and rescued wounded people, taking them to the closest hospital or village clinic. I stayed in Kitui alone. Going to the bush churches and navigating dangerous territory affected me. I was barely able to tolerate the blistering heat and food, which the people so generously shared with us.

We slept on dirt floors with pigs and chickens, with extended family members in one room. During the time it took for Zack to deal with and advise in difficult church matters, I felt it was best I held the fort at home.

I was fearful. Being home alone was immediately known in an African setting. Gangs of men roamed the area and broke into homes, raping women and children and stealing possessions. We did

Uncurling Freedom

not own many things, but to people trapped in poverty, anything they steal can be sold for a meal.

All our windows and outside doors had metal bars, and our dogs stayed inside as my early warning system. We also had several dogs outside. Even with this security, raiders fed the dogs poisoned meat, so they could easily gain access to our compound. We eventually paid for a security company to protect us. We pressed a button, and armed guards appeared at our gate. I had to do this several times.

Even with these measures in place, I was fearful. Was God's work so important that Zack had to travel such distances to take care of it? I read a lot, and every morning studied my Bible, but a lurking fear always lingered.

Zack and the Roof Fall:

Diani graduated from Moody Bible Institute on May 11, 1996, and Zack fell off the church roof almost at the same time. I was in the USA at her graduation when the news came. Frantic arrangements were made

Uncurling Freedom

to change flight tickets and gain some idea from our Kenya doctor of the damage.

After my arrival in Nairobi, I asked Pastor Luka, "What happened with Zack falling off the roof?"

Pastor met me in the hospital hallway and explained, "Zack and the work crew were installing corrugated iron sheets on the roof of the church building. It started to rain and Mzee (polite name for Zack-old man) told everyone to get off the roof. Immediately Mzee was skidding down the wet roof. In seconds he had to decide and brace himself for a landing. As he slid down he tried to get a hold of protruding bolts, but only lacerated his hands. He landed on the short side of the building, in a sand pit on both feet. His knees crushed into his chest. We ran up the short hill to help him, but when we got there we thought he was dead. He was only winded. We started to pick him up."

Zack said, "Do not do that. Go find an old door, bring it here and I will tell you how to get me onto it."

Uncurling Freedom

The crew organized and once Zack was on the door the question was, "How do we get him to the hospital?"

No one could drive Zack's pick up, so Pastor Luka ran to the market and found a vehicle and driver belonging to Father Paddy of the Catholic diocese. They loaded him up and drove to the local hospital. Thankfully a visiting doctor from Ireland was there and made the decision that they should take him to Nairobi Hospital.

Father Paddy said, "They do not have proper equipment here to determine damage to the spine and internal organs, and we need to get him to Nairobi as soon as possible."

They loaded Zack on his door, and Father Paddy headed out into the hazardous Kenyan night. No highway bandits appeared, nor speeding vehicles. On the way Zack said, "I need to urinate, please" so Father Paddy stopped and opened the van door to facilitate Zack relieving himself.

Arriving at A&E Nairobi Hospital, he was almost dropped by the orderlies when they took him out

Uncurling Freedom

of the van. Screaming, Zack said, "Do not grab my broken foot." This brought many curious faces to the open windows.

An orthopedic surgeon was called who tried to manually manipulate the badly crushed foot. This was a disaster. A different surgeon then operated, inserting plates and screws into one foot. The right foot was badly cracked, so they decided to immobilize it with plaster of Paris. Zack's L5 vertebrae were also crushed.

He spent three weeks in the hospital. Then we were taken by ambulance to a friend's house, where Zack lay on his back for six months. These friends were on "home assignment" so we had the use of their house.

All activity was done on his back. Absolutely no other movement was allowed. The Kitui church project continued with contractor Gil and Steve and Pastor Luka.

My roles multiplied. I became caretaker, nurse, purchaser, transporter of all building materials and relief food, business manager and driver. We were feeding 30 pastors and their families while providing education funds to 25 children.

Uncurling Freedom

Zack drew plans on his chest for all the doors and windows, and I delivered them to the site. This was three hours one way. I obtained help purchasing food and materials but drove that dangerous way myself. My goal was to get back to Nairobi before dusk while gripping the steering wheel and staring into the setting sun. I asked myself, "Will I make it before dark?"

After six months, Zack was allowed up and taught to walk again with the help of crutches.

'"Come," Jesus said. Then Peter got down out of the boat, walked on the water and came toward Jesus. But when he saw the wind, he was afraid and, beginning to sink, cried out, "Lord, save me!"' (Matthew 14:29-30 JBP).

I am a defender. All my life my hand reaches out for a hand to clasp mine on the journey. Who will clasp it? Who will hold up my hands? I have held so many hands up. There was no one else. I had to hold my own hands up.

In every way imaginable, I was overwhelmed by Zack's injury and all the needs of the Kitui people and the church project. For six months I ran on fumes. I was

Uncurling Freedom

drained physically and emotionally, barely hanging on by a tattered thread. I needed reminding and admonishing to "Not look at the waves, but to look up." I had to remember God saw my tears and shared my pain. He was with me.

Death of Alice:

Our co-workers, Clive and Mary, British missionaries in Kenya were compelled by the devastating child abandonment in Kenya to start New Life Home. They needed assistance with accounting and organizing the child sponsorship program they had set up for pastors' children. When they needed a break, a friend and I would take over management of the home.

As we had only one car, I was able to hitch a ride to Nairobi on a petrol tanker. Our Indian neighbor went every day to collect petrol, diesel and oil. My seat was in the middle on the hot engine. On arrival my buttocks were flaming red-hot. When my work in Nairobi was done, I would arrange a pick up back to Kitui, taking work for New Life with me.

Uncurling Freedom

The newborn babies in this home were abandoned in pit latrines, on the roadside and even in hospitals. Mothers simply walked away and left their babies. New Life provided excellent care for every rescued child. It was a true honor to save these little ones who had been left out in the cold to die.

I was on assignment for three weeks at New Life when Alice arrived on our doorstep with AIDS. She lay in her crib, her little eyes searching for my face as I held her minute-sized hand, her cheeks hardly bigger than a silver dollar.

The doctors tried fruitlessly to insert an IV in her arm for a blood transfusion while I held her little body. She lasted three weeks. Every day I touched her body, felt her chest and heart pounding, thundering through her nightgown, searching for each breath. Her struggle for life dwindled.

The Lord God Almighty opened his arms, his heart and his heaven, and took this little "wisp of a life" quietly to himself in her sleep. In those final weeks of her life, she was cherished, fed, clothed and prayed for.

Uncurling Freedom

I took her little hand and said my final Kwaheri (good-bye). I was not able to add the usual African Salute, "Yakuonana" (We shall meet again face to face), as I was not sure I would see her again here on earth.

My emotions and heart forever changed for the children of Africa because I touched Alice. But more effectually, she touched me. Given the opportunity, who can know the extent of a child's life touching this world? That one child could ignite a continent, become a president, teacher, doctor or parent.

I know I am different having known her. As I remember her again, my heart continues to weep. But I also rejoice, because through her many other children have been reached. During this time, children became part of my being.

Did we go to Kitui to build churches, water tanks, irrigation—or to touch children? I have seen with my own eyes my own transformation.

Uncurling Freedom

SOUTH SUDAN

Why Sudan?

"When we left Kenya in 2007, I thought God was done with me," said Lorna.

God said, "*No, a little dab of paint is needed here. A line here, some adjustments to your face and much more to your life.*"

My life was like a painting of the Lord. Part of this painting necessarily took me to South Sudan where much more refining was needed. Trauma, violence, caring for the war-wounded, and learning to eat rice and beans for two years.

In Hudson Taylor's "Spiritual Secret," he talks about the testing experiences he went through. They tempered his heart to strengthen it and helped him be

Uncurling Freedom

more patient with others who had suffered more, lost more. To encourage thousands, he suffered through childlike trust and testing, in order to learn the deeper lessons of our Father's loving care. Difficulties and deliverances came, which made lifelong blessings from the results of such pain.

Such pain growing up fatherless, and being a parent to my siblings and alcoholic mother. Learning how to trust God to provide for our family and even to attend school. Living with a step-father who beat up Mum and tormented us, especially my crippled brother, Claude Louis. He was thrown off the house steps, but survived. Separated as a family and sent to different countries. Each and every trial in my life produced "flowers" for God's picking. Each lesson spurred me on the journey and carved resilience into my soul. I would make it because God was with me, carrying me.

In May 2007, thoughts of retiring crossed our minds. When we were in the United Kingdom visiting my dying brother Claude Louis, we received a call from Roland. We attended Nairobi chapel with him, and he

Uncurling Freedom

was a part of our home group as well as an amazing pilot with Mission Aviation Fellowship (MAF).

Before leaving Kenya, I said to him, "Roland, I really do not want to leave my country." His call explained the need at the Akot Medical Mission in South Sudan.

Did God want us to hear the appeal for help? Was this an excuse for not leaving Africa?

Thousands of southern Sudanese women, children and young men drifted in the wilderness. They dodged rape, threats of human trafficking and annihilation. They ate leaves and roots of unknown plants to live one more day. Had God forgotten them?

Living on the equator, the dark blue-black skin of the Sudanese helps them endure the equatorial sun. Their tall majestic figures effectively disperse heat. They smile through somber and distrusting eyes. These are a people, concealing millennia of war and abuse. A people with no medical care.

If I had the opportunity to give my life to help save a survivor who is broken into so many pieces—a people who are not sure who they are, would I do this?

Uncurling Freedom

Yes, I would reach out, not as an excuse to remain in Africa, but as a believer. Because their pain became mine. I must imitate the Master Giver.

Before making our decision, we were invited by Bill of Mustard Seed International to visit Akot Medical Mission, to see the project. We travelled in a 14-seat plane with Africa Inland Mission (AIMAIR), landing on a dirt runway strewn with grazing cattle and mud puddles. Naked children ran happily alongside our little plane.

Bill asked, "Have you made a decision about coming in January?"

"Yes. Although neither of us has medical experience, we will come and assist at the hospital."

At first we did not experience culture shock, as this was where we were meant to be. My son, Elior said to me, "Mum, this is an African adventure and you can meet the challenge, as you have done so many times serving in Kenya. Even in your old age."

Since we had been missionaries in Kenya for 36 years, we thought going to Sudan would be a piece of cake. But when we took a bite out of that cake, we were

Uncurling Freedom

not prepared for the taste. After two and a half years, we decided to leave that traumatic life.

Trauma brought on by war and violence. We never knew when the Sudan Peoples Liberation Army would break into our hospital, shoot us all and ravage the compound. One time, they arrived on vehicles with rocket-propelled grenades and demanded we fill up their water tanks.

Before we came to Akot, we traveled through Kenya where the country was in the midst of post-election violence. Roadblocks, ranting crowds and anger overflowed the streets. We went through a country in upheaval to another country in worse condition.

"We all stumble in many ways" (James 3:2 JBP). But falling down isn't what makes me a failure. It's staying down!

Get back up, dust yourself off, receive God's grace, learn from the experience, and move on.

I needed to stop beating myself up about Sudan. How could I run away from these hurting, needy people? How would they survive? Where would they

Uncurling Freedom

get medicine? I felt like a coward. I should have been able to withstand such torture. After all, the precious Sudanese people had survived for decades.

People:

In our lifetimes, we come face to face with so many interesting people. South Sudan was no exception. Everyone has a unique story, each one more painful that the last. For those people I have written about, I wanted and needed their sadness, their trauma and resilience to reach my heart. For that time period, it would guide me in my interaction with them, and hopefully teach me how to be a different person.

Old man in the Fire:

A frantic messenger arrived at Akot Medical Mission, rushing all over the hospital trying to find Zack. When he found Zack, he said, "Please Mzee, can you come quickly? An old man has fallen in the fire, and he is badly burned on his feet and face. There is no one to help him, and there is no vehicle to bring him to the hospital."

Uncurling Freedom

Zack said, "Of course! I will come right now. Show us where this man lives."

God blessed our hospital with two Toyota land cruisers. These vehicles took us everywhere to help needy people. Zack and one of our male Kenyan nurses rushed off into the bush to find the old man. He was having seizures, falling into the fire with no one to pull him out. He was in a terrible condition, and his treatment was on-going for months. We only had topical antibiotics and gauze bandages to manage his extensive burns.

As we shared daily devotions, this man grew spiritually. When it came time for him to leave the hospital, he refused to leave. He was fed, medically taken care of and was with people who cared for his well-being. His wife had left him as another man took her to be his wife. There was no reason for this man to return home. He sat on the hospital pathway and shared his healing story with anyone passing by.

Being elderly in Sudan has its own complexities. Old people were often taken into the forest, put into a hole and covered with sand, leaving

Uncurling Freedom

only their heads above ground. They were left for the wild animals to devour. No compassion. No caring.

I wanted to do all I could for these desperate people and not devour God's provision entrusted to me.

Daniel:

He was one of our hospital care workers. One day, Daniel asked me, "Can you come and visit me at my home and see my grandmother?"

"Of course! You just plan when to take the journey."

Up to this time, Daniel had kept me at arm's length, and I wondered why. I was soon to find out, but never understood his story. When Daniel was a child, Arabs from North Sudan raided his village. The Janjaweed are an Arab militia comprised of camel herders. The Sudanese president used them to mastermind a plot to wipe out African tribes in a campaign of murder, rape and deportation.

Daniel dug a hole and burrowed into it to hide and wait out the killing. When he finally came out of

Uncurling Freedom

his hole, he could hardly walk. He was emaciated, and in terror.

He said, "When I looked for my parents and relatives, no one was alive. Only broken bodies. The rest they bound and carried away." Gigantic tears filled his cheeks.

After work one day, we set off through inches of deep dust and heat haze. Accompanying us were frisky, wild long-horned cattle and their keepers. The Dinka Cattle Keepers are boys who dust their bodies and faces with gray ash as protection against flies and lethal malarial mosquitoes, but also considered a mark of beauty. Covered with this ash and up to seven feet, six inches tall, the Dinka were referred to as "gentle" or "ghostly" giants by the early explorers. The Dinka call themselves "jieng" and "mony-jang," which means "men of men."

An army of grey and magnificent regal ghosts, all carrying AK-47 rifles, cattle and dust surrounded us. These ghosts obstructed our way forward with childish curiosity. It was not every day these ruffian cattle keepers saw mzungus (whites) tramping in the bush.

Uncurling Freedom

We were not afraid. Daniel was with us. Actually it was exciting.

The only sounds were our breathing and shuffling feet through the sand — only Daniel, Zack and I.

It was natural to wonder, "Am I heading into danger?" in a country where ambush is commonplace.

On arrival we sat on the hot dirt and were served okra by Daniel's shriveled, toothless, yet sweet grandmother. Hugging is not a custom in Sudan, but I am sure if I hugged her, she would have splintered into pieces.

Terror burrowed into Daniel, his place of retreat, shelter and refuge. In this place he hid himself from the outside world, suddenly manifesting in explosive anger and unreasonable demands on us. He had no frame of reference to manage his inner turmoil nor anyone to share it with. All his people suffered from this stalking terror.

Somehow he and I connected, but I had no frame of reference to understand his pain, no matter how many books I read by Sudanese experts.

Uncurling Freedom

Each person who suffers trauma is unique in the pain, and each person will understand differently. For me it was a fragile walk into his heart and eyes. We both somehow knew that a measure of understanding existed between us.

I lay hands on him for the healing of his damaged soul and spirit. His Bible was burnt in the rampage and destruction by the army.

Then I flew away to another safer land and left him there suffering. As I boarded the small MAF plane, Daniel stood in the dust and our eyes met in a final kwaheri (goodbye).

I left my heart and Bible with him, with this promise from Luke 22:31, 32. Jesus praying for Peter not to be sifted as wheat, but to be saved and changed. As such, the ability to bring such healing to those around Daniel in Akot and his Dinka tribe. He would be a peacemaker, shining with the glory of God to his people.

I wonder where you are today, Daniel.

Uncurling Freedom

Mzee Gideon:

Gideon served as a Clinical Officer under the British colonial office in Sudan. These are licensed practitioners of medicine who are trained and authorized to perform general or specialized medical duties such as: diagnosis and treatment of disease and injury, ordering and interpreting medical tests, performing routine medical and surgical procedures and referring patients to other practitioners.

Gideon's wisdom in dealing with all tribal issues in the hospital was priceless. He also tempered us "outsiders" in how to live with the Dinka and Nuer people. We knew nothing about their traditions and customs. Our team was comprised of three expatriate Kenyan male nurses, Zack and I, and 40 general hospital staff.

Coming from the "first world" we tended to prance around in the "Know-better-than-you-do" attitude. We took over and did things our way in this "third world" although these people had survived millennia without us.

Uncurling Freedom

Gideon would say, "But Madam/Sir" and proceed to show us how things were done in the Sudan bush. He was always right. After all, he had survived decades in Sudan. Who better to show us the way? Yet for us expats, it was hard to listen to this wise and gentle old man. We thought modern technology outweighed their rural traditions of survival living.

I was truly humbled and said, "Yes, Gideon, you are right." But how often did I say that? I was far too proud and arrogant. If only I could go back and sit at his feet again.

Gideon's presence at the hospital brought stability in every situation. Since he was so very old when we met him, no doubt he now sits at his Savior's feet, joining his ancestors in their eternal rest.

Rose The Bread Maker:

She organized all the cooking for our staff and also maintained the hospital buildings. Rose came from Western Equatoria to serve us, leaving her family in safety with her husband, who was an Adventist, pastor.

Uncurling Freedom

Bread was a delicacy we had only tasted in our dreams. When we shopped monthly in Rumbek, 30 miles away, Rose collected yeast, flour and sugar. All the food supplies, including the ingredients for our bread, came by road from Khartoum, a journey of 634 miles that wound through hostile tribes and terrain. Ah, the wonder in eating it!

All our cooking was done outdoors with wood. Zack and his crew foraged in the forests for fallen trees, brought them back and cut them into manageable pieces. We had no ovens, so Rose arranged hot coals on top of which she laid a large metal lid and buns, then covered them with a cooking pot.

Everyone hung around the fire waiting for a bun. When they were ready, we each ate one with a cup of boiling sweet milky tea. Each bite was savored, as it would be a long time before the next baking day.

Now I am no longer able to eat bread or rice and beans, because of the damage that food did to my stomach.

I still miss the smells, smiles, black dark faces, bare feet and sharing of life with these amazing

Uncurling Freedom

Sudanese people. Out in that distant place, we were best friends.

Evacuating a Hemorrhaging Mother:

Mary Immaculate DOR Hospital is situated in Mapuordit, approximately 76 kilometers from Rumbek, the provincial capital of Lakes State in Southern Sudan. Obstetric Fistula Surgery is done at the hospital, free of charge by a specialist surgeon. This surgery repairs obstetric fistula, an unnatural connection related to childbirth. Sudanese girls are married off by ten and immediately become pregnant.

Days of unrelieved labor creates compression which may cut off the blood supply to the baby and to the mother's internal soft tissues, causing both to die. The dead tissue results in holes (fistula) in the walls separating the woman's reproductive and excretory systems.

So after losing her baby, a woman must live with a never-ending flow of urine and/or feces that destroys her life. If one of these girls survives, she will live her life with the ugly label of "Modern Day Leper."

Uncurling Freedom

The smell of an uncontrollable and unending flow of waste obviously carries terrible social implications. For a woman or a girl with fistula, a lack of understanding of the condition has dire consequences.

Her community will nearly always ostracize her. In many cases, her husband will leave her or send her back to her family. In the worst cases, even her family will abandon her, leaving her to fend for herself. The bright eyes and giant smile she once owned are replaced by the pain and loneliness only a leper can know.

In the pouring rain, Ann, a young expectant mother arrived, hemorrhaging terribly. Blood was everywhere. As we had no surgical facilities, the Kenyan nurses decided to move Ann to Mapurodit hospital, 30 miles from our location.

Thus began a journey of hope for the woman and her unborn baby. We placed her into our Toyota pickup, and Zack attached her IV to a nail in the roof. It was my job to make sure the IV stayed in place. Its liquid-life flowing into her veins was critical to her

Uncurling Freedom

survival, so we had to maintain its flow over the two-hour drive.

Imagine swishing through potholes the size of small lakes. Water poured over our hood and the entire vehicle slid from side to side. At times, some of the potholes were filled with felled trees, which gave vehicles additional traction. We did not know if we would sink to the other side of the world or drive out of it. Each pothole was a new challenge.

With much praise we arrived at the hospital, and Ann was rushed into surgery for a C-Section. Mother and child survived.

In Sudan, questions and challenges always appeared. "Will we arrive with no issues from gun-running rebels and Cattle Keepers?" These wild hunters were always on the lookout for what they could "harvest" from people on any journey to any place. If we arrived without incident, we shouted a great "Hallelujah!"

But then, we faced the return journey. Somewhat less stressed, we were completely exhausted by heat, dehydration and the lack of food for twelve hours.

Six a.m. Reveille on the Airstrip:

Before my early morning wake up, I carried my bed outside the boiling hot building. The roofs were made of corrugated iron sheets. A day in the sun turned our room into an oven. No doubt we could bake bread in that room. Wouldn't that be a lovely aroma — tea and bread.

Temperatures rose above 110 degrees. Zack was concerned about me sleeping under the stars in case a snake visited in the night or cozied up for the coolness of my wet towel.

Many nights, as I lay with a wet towel covering my body, I looked up into the sky. It reminded me of Psalm 66:5, *"Take a good look at God's wonders. They will take your breath away"* (JBP).

As I looked up at the stars I thought, *On the other side of those glittering dots, God is looking down on me. My children and grandies see those same stars.*

Uncurling Freedom

The Star-Keeper kept me safe out there in the cool dark. His voice of love beamed down through the eyes of each of those blinking stars.

My alarm was set for five a.m. I awoke in the dark, and found my way to the kitchen. I wanted to make a thermos of tea. Then I headed to the office to check the internet, read my Bible and pray. In the dark, I dressed and walked with my headlamp to the small runway. It was time for my six a.m. walk, which proved most interesting.

Why on earth would I go out this early in South Sudan? Because it was the coolest time for 24 hours. Not long into my walk I heard puffs and sighs behind me. I looked back and saw a sheet of black across the runway.

Then the sheet reached me. One hundred black Sudanese Army men with their AK-47 guns jogged beside me. With a sigh of relief, I kept going. With them I was truly safe. Who would ever attack me?

We exchanged greetings. Then came a hoard of starving feral dogs, dashing and snarling all around us.

I yelled, "Get thee behind me!"

Uncurling Freedom

They stopped, perplexed, with heads askew. It seemed they were questioning me, *What is this white person saying?* They only understood Dinka.

By the tone and strength of my voice the dogs were alert for action. They finally realized I would not back down. Tails fell between their back legs and they darted away.

I heaved a sigh of relief. *That really worked.* Then I continued my peaceful walk.

A huge red sun came up over the dry landscape. The day would be sweltering again.

After that first encounter on the airstrip with the Sudanese Army and feral dogs, we each knew our place. Early morning walks became a comfort.

A Blazing Village:

An issue arose between the Sudan People's Liberation Army and the Cattle Keepers. The slightest problem might cause an all-out war. One Cattle Keeper was shot. In retaliation, other Cattle Keepers raided the army barracks half a mile from our hospital. They killed

Uncurling Freedom

the army commander and 19 soldiers. The situation was suddenly ten times worse.

The Cattle Keepers were told, "You bring those responsible for shooting our men. If you fail to bring them, we will come and eat all your cows."

Such a threat to a Dinka tribesman results in war, because cows are like cash. Cows are also a source of friction — first with neighboring clans in the same tribe, then with other tribes or with anyone who says, "We will come and eat your cows."

The Dinka, the dominant tribe in the South Sudan, regard cattle as sacred, approximating human beings in value. They live in synergy with their cows, sleeping outdoors in the same camp. The Dinka use the cow's milk, blood, skin and waste as vital resources for survival. One clan's herd can be as large as 1,000. At night, a cattle camp may house over 10,000 cows.

The Cattle Keepers brought one man to take the blame for the shooting. He was shot right before their eyes. The Dinka retaliated, and more army men were killed.

Uncurling Freedom

Blinding war and fire erupted in our village of Akot. Many people disappeared into the bush. The army barricaded our town. They marched from house to house, pillaging. What they could not carry away, they burned.

People did not have time to save anything from their homes. They lost everything and many lost their lives. Those who were injured on both sides were taken into the bush. No one came to the hospital for treatment. If it were known that the Army or the Dinka Cattle Keepers were patients, the hospital would have been raided and the injured killed in their bed along with other innocent patients.

To further complicate everything, The Magician, a powerful witch doctor, planned to come to Akot to sacrifice a ritual cow. This chief's visit added to the mayhem and the killing.

I wondered what 10,000 cows and their Cattle Keepers might look like on our airstrip.

Gunshots were everywhere in many directions. Rocket-propelled grenades sat on trucks which rolled down the runway. The Army faced off the Cattle

Uncurling Freedom

Keepers and tormented ordinary villagers. Many sought refuge at the hospital, bringing what few items and animals they could collect before running to us. People were strewn all over the hospital on porches and passageways. These hurting and bedraggled humans suffered such terror.

Outside our gate, an innocent passerby was caught by the Army and beaten to death. We heard his death cries. His body was left in the road for dogs and the sun to consume. The Army trooped into our compound. At gunpoint, they marched the women and children who had taken refuge with us, outside the gate. They were forced to sit in the dirt as they were interrogated about their male relatives' whereabouts.

Would we be next?

Colonel Billy (US Retired Army Special Forces) lived on our compound and often dressed in his fatigues. He knew the names of top officials and rattled them off. Soon the drunk, drugged and filthy Army men faded into the bush. Without the help of Colonel Billy, all those people would have been killed.

Uncurling Freedom

After four days, a contingent of Army, police and wildlife officials arrived. They secured our compound with armed soldiers. The United Nations Security Council marched in with food, clothing and medical supplies. Slowly, people started the return journeys to their homes, knowing they would find only ash and destruction.

A people with no hope, these were also a people who knew how to rise out of the fire and keep going. "Hatua kwa hatua" (Kiswahili) one step at a time. From those very ashes, they would build again.

The Muslim extremists of northern Sudan continued to supply arms to all the tribes around us, which caused continual instability.

To this day, any noise behind me or a touch on my shoulder sends me into spiraling shock.

Evacuating Zack:

Zack scraped a toe on a metal piece at the hospital. It soon became inflamed, badly infected and continued to swell. Although he took oral antibiotics,

Uncurling Freedom

no improvement was noticeable. He was unable to walk and had to keep his right leg elevated.

After a month without improvement, I talked with our Kenyan doctor who was appalled that Zack was not on IV antibiotics. Infections of such duration, especially in the tropics, posed serious problems. He was moving toward gangrene or blood poisoning (septicemia). Our doctor demanded Zack's immediate evacuation from South Sudan.

As I was in Kenya at the time, the race was on to locate flights coming to Kenya from South Sudan. Mission Aviation fellowship (MAF) and Africa Inland Mission (AIMAIR) serve the missionary community in east and central Africa. We had to find a plane coming to Kenya that would stop off at Akot and pick up Zack.

Being such a remote area, I had to make A, B and C contingency plans. AIMAIR responded to the plea. We never knew the actual ETA until the plane arrived. Satellite phone and radio contact were constantly maintained.

Once Zack knew the ETA, he asked the Kenyan nurses to drive down to the army barracks to inform

Uncurling Freedom

them of the plane's arrival. The Army camouflaged themselves in bushes bordering the airstrip. As soon as the plane landed, armored vehicles surrounded the entire area. They needed to make sure the plane was not carrying guns or rebels.

The pilot spent the night, and at daybreak he and Zack walked to the airstrip for an early departure. With much chagrin they found it blanketed in dense, unusual fog. Departure was delayed until the sun broke the fog in masses of small plumes, sufficient enough to taxi on and lift into the blue sky.

The destination was Lokichogio (Loki), a bustling town 30 kilometers from the South Sudan border. Loki hosted the United Nations offices (part of the Operation Lifeline Sudan program) and 49 non-government organizations, as well a large orthopedic hospital run by the International Committee of the Red Cross.

I had arranged for The Flying Doctors /AMREF (Africa Medical and Research Foundation) to be in Loki by 11 a.m. Since I was in Nairobi, the Flying Doctors were in Loki (northern Kenya) while Zack was

Uncurling Freedom

in Akot, South Sudan — the feasibility of the plan coming together was beyond imagination. Without satellite and radio communication, we would have stumbled in the dark. The air ambulance was time-barred, as they had other emergency calls to deal with.

In the nick of time the AIMAIR plane landed in Loki. Parking alongside the Flying Doctor's plane, the outstanding Medivac nurses transferred Zack, took care of his immigration documents, and connected him to IV medication. They treated him for the serious infection and prepared him for shock while in flight.

I received all these communications by phone. Once I knew the Nairobi ETA, I walked for one hour to reach Wilson Airport. I was there when the plane landed and accompanied the road ambulance to Nairobi Hospital. What excitement to drive on the wrong side of the road with flashing lights and sirens!

Doctor Paul said, "Thank you, Lorna, for arranging this journey. His infection is serious, and Zack could have lost his leg. It could have become gangrenous or he could have had blood poisoning (septicemia)."

Uncurling Freedom

It took many days for the infection to be treated. When Zack healed, we traveled back to South Sudan, where many more Sudanese needed medical care and food assistance.

Crystal Scars:

Mental health is triggered by PTSD trauma. This disorder is characterized by failure to recover after experiencing or witnessing a terrifying event. After some counseling recommendation, it was suggested I look into a disorder that might complicate my life. I researched Complex-PTSD disorder.

For 51 years, I lived with a so-called Christian husband who was emotionally and verbally abusive on a daily basis. Not only did it wear down my self-esteem, but it also impacted my nervous system in the same way physical trauma does. Long after the abuse occurred, memories produced negative feelings, penetrating substantial aches, along with negative thoughts about myself.

C-PTSD is a condition that results from chronic long-term exposure to unseen emotional and verbal abuse. I had little or no control over my situation with little or no hope of escape. I felt bad about myself and hated to look into the mirror. There I could see my sorrow and the ugliness this trauma caused. Shame and depression dogged my steps.

This shame continually tormented me. It led to self-punishment and denial with absolutely no self-worth. Shame grew in the silence of darkness and held me back. My feet were stuck in rocks, unable to move forward. Consequently I never expressed wanting anything, because I felt non-existent. The shame was never- ending. Nothing ever changed.

C-PTSD causes hidden wounds of depression, anxiety, confusion, exclusion, avoidance, a sense of persecution, seeing danger everywhere, and being a lifelong helper/enabler. Essentially "Complex" describes how one trauma layer can interact with another.

What it has done to me:
- Exhaustion, tension in my body, constantly feeling tired for no reason.

Uncurling Freedom

- Emotional shifts. No matter how much I give, it is never enough. Yet I have increased levels of anger, irritability, resentment and cynicism.
- Thought patterns such as: Is any of this effective? Am I making any difference?
- Behavioral shifts, avoidance of relationships with everyone.
- Relationship changes, seeing danger everywhere, a sense of persecution or martyrdom.
- Personal antagonism, shame, guilt.
- Significantly higher risk of suicide. For many years, I have wanted to end it all.

It has left me feeling isolated and worthless, depressed and thoroughly worn out from constantly being on guard for the next attack. I have become so withdrawn, I stand outside myself looking at me—a person who is so different from what I was created to be.

Uncurling Freedom

I was told, "Mum, when Dad comes you act so differently than when you are just with us."

Dorothy said, "I see a different you when you step away and come out of your hiding, away from your reservation around people. You are so funny. As soon as Zack enters the room you slink back under your shell."

Looking back over my life and years, several incidents caused this condition. After my father died, I slept with a gun under my pillow to protect my siblings and alcoholic mother. I was only 13.

When my daughter was two months old, Zack threw us out of our car in Nairobi and forced me to walk miles back home. He was not held accountable, so I continually relived this pain. Then we went to South Sudan.

In a message from Bill Johnson-Bethel, he quoted these words: "I am not going to remove the scars from your life, but I am going to arrange them where they have the appearance of carving on a fine piece of crystal." - Dick Joyce.

Uncurling Freedom

It is from these scars that I must write. Were I to remain silent and not share my pain and scars, I would be hoarding my pain. This denial would eventually lead to my internal destruction, demise by my own hand.

Gideon was told, *"Go in the strength you have and I will save Israel and be with you"* (Judges 6:14 KJV).

A key lesson for me is how my pain can become my greatest asset. This struggle in understanding and application is on-going. I have always been strong enough. But being strong gets harder with unending years of constant wearing down.

Ann asked me, "How have you been able to hold on for so long?"

I shook my head. "There must be a steel rod up my spine holding me together, helping me survive life and my marriage."

One day, I told Philo, "I have never strayed or been tempted by drugs, allowed missionary men to hit on me, lived as an alcoholic or been unfaithful. If you had a different mother, you would not be the person you are."

Uncurling Freedom

Thought-provoking silence was his response.

Paul said, "When you were treated badly by Zack, it was expected, as in your youth. It was no different from your past, so you took the abuse and carried on. You did not know he should have been held accountable."

Diana said, "I love your son, Philo. He has so many of your mannerism, expressions and spiritual qualities."

Then I realized Philo's giftedness is part of the lost me. When I look at his life, I see so much of who I could have been, but it has been lost, buried and trampled within my marital journey.

I am so thankful God planted in Philo's life many of my own characteristics and quest for God. At least that created part of me lives on in him, my other children and all my grandchildren. It did not end with me.

Uncurling Freedom

Uncurling Freedom

A TRIBUTE TO CLAUDE LOUIS

His was a face that when the angels looked at him, they smiled. Claude Louis, my brother. He was born in Dar-es-Salaam, Tanganyika, German East Africa in 1943 (now Tanzania) in the German hospital to Luc Bertie and Hélène, my parents.

Later, after my brother Anthony's birth, Mum and we three children traveled by steamer to Victoria, Mahe, Seychelles Islands to see her father Fernande. With no port to dock in, we climbed down a ladder to a small rowboat, then sailed to the island to see my grandfather.

I was only five and wondered what my grandfather would be like. Would he even speak the

Uncurling Freedom

same language? Later, I found out he spoke French, Creole and English.

Mum held my hand and I looked at her. Such a beauty: blue eyes like the ocean, raven black hair, and a ravishing face. In that moment I was no longer afraid. She brushed away the cobwebs of my insecurity.

We then sailed to Lourenco Marques, The Pearl of the Indian Ocean, (Maputo) Mozambique. At the time, it was Portuguese East Africa. I have no memory of the onward journey to Broken Hill, (Kitwe) Northern Rhodesia (Zambia).

During that time, my dad worked in the Copper Belt in deep underground mining for lead, zinc and copper. At Christmas the Zulus danced around our house, asking for presents. My dad, as the kind and generous person he was, gave them something. Then off they went to the next house. Later I learned these Zulus were friends and not the horrible Africans.

While in Broken Hill, a polio epidemic broke out. Claude Louis was playing by a window, and brother Anthony pushed him out. He fell and cut his leg. The complications of the injury, along with the

Uncurling Freedom

alcoholic surgeon and the polio caused him to lose the use of one leg. Sadness settled on his face, framed by straight blond hair, and deep-set brown, gentle cow-like eyes. The expression lasted his whole life. He became a punching bag for anyone who took aim at him.

Many years later I asked him, "Claude Louis, what went through your mind as you were falling out that window?"

He said, "Oh no, I'm going to break something."

"Did you blame your brother for causing that fall?"

"I have never thought about it. Later in life Anthony told me how terrible it made him feel to be the person who caused my injury."

"So, for the rest of your life, you were a cripple. How did that affect you?"

He thought a moment, then said, "It was hard because first of all I had no calipers. I had to walk on my hands and knees. Later when dad could afford calipers, I had to lug around my heavy metal-braced leg."

Uncurling Freedom

"How were you treated in boarding school?"

"The Brits and South African kids were very unkind to a cripple. They made fun of me and taunted me, because they knew I couldn't catch up with them. They ran off laughing."

"Did you like school?" I asked.

Claude Louis said, "Yes, but living was hell. I only saw Mum and Dad every three months as they lived too far away to come and see us."

While working in the mines, Dad became ill with lead poisoning. Breathing lead in those depths damaged all his organs, the brain, kidneys and stomach. It was during this time my two sisters were born. Christine was born in Broken Hill and Betty in Ndola.

Dad's body slowly shriveled up, so we had to head back to Kenya. We hoped our extended family would help us when they saw the condition Dad was in.

He was able to work for a few years in Voi, Kenya, constructing a water pipeline from Mzima Springs to Mombasa. His body continued deteriorating as his lungs were eaten up. Breathing became a challenge. Eventually, internal bleeding was also a

Uncurling Freedom

problem. His brother Worth decided to send him to England for treatment.

It was too late. I held my littlest sister Betty's hand, barely three years old as we stood at the East Leigh airport in Nairobi. We watched Dad fly away.

Sending Dad off for treatment bewildered and crushed us, as we knew we would never see him again. Mum was a life-long alcoholic with various mental issues.

After Dad died, we lived in a derelict hotel in Nairobi. I was a mother to my mother at 13 and a mother to my four siblings. My brothers were out of control. Anthony was put into a boarding school. Claude Louis was taken to Seychelles by my mother's brother and treated with such inhumanity it even surprised the villagers.

My grandfather, Fernande, brought treats and cared for Claude Louis when he could, but Uncle Leslie treated Claude Louise as he did Mum — with banishment. Claude Louis was tied to a tree by his good leg and cowered in the shade. This cruel man was a

Uncurling Freedom

Navy Captain, awarded the Order of the British Empire medal.

How is it possible to have two such opposite characteristics in one person?

Claude Louis eventually returned to Kenya and fell into all sorts of trouble. We had no home and no family. He was sent to a reform school, the only white person there, with over 600 wild African boys. Considered a half-caste by the colonial government, it was natural Claude Louis would be delegated to that place of horror. More of his soul eroded.

How can we do such things to each other?
One person becomes more acceptable than another because of the color of skin, hair, size of nose, et cetera.

A missionary lady, Kooth, who loved my family and did not see any color bar, took me to visit Claude Louis at the reform school. Our whole family was white, several blonde and blue-eyed, several with black, straight hair. The internal struggle for all us children was trying to prove we were white. Living life as white people, but treated as if we were black — the untouchables. Living in the silence, shame and hiding.

Uncurling Freedom

What I failed to do for Claude Louis has plagued me for years. I was given a scholarship to attend Bible school in the USA. So I left him and Anthony to fend for themselves in England.

After Dad died, Mum remarried a man with six children, making a total of 11 children at the house. The stepfather was a beast. He beat Mum and us, threw my crippled brother down the stairs, fed and clothed only his own children. More rampage, locked doors, trying to survive.

I worked at babysitting jobs to buy us socks or undies.

Kenya would soon gain their independence. Our Australian caseworker, Mr. Rigs, worked with the Kenya Child Welfare Society. He decided to remove my sisters and brothers from my mother.

By court order, my sisters were adopted by a couple who were supposedly Christians from the church we attended. They were taken to England. My brothers were taken to London, and dropped off with some money and a place to live to fend for themselves. Mr. Rigs wanted to get all the children out of Kenya

Uncurling Freedom

before independence so they would not become streetwalkers and vagabonds.

Miraculously, I was able to find Claude Louis. We would stop over on our way to and from Kenya to see him. The first time I found him, he was living with a woman and her four children in an abandoned hotel in London. It was such a dangerous place we had to sleep with our passports and money strapped to our bodies. After so many years, he was excited to see me. The loathsome place we slept held no significance to seeing his face again.

Before I found Claude Louis again, he had married a prostitute and fathered a little boy. Due to his violence and drinking, his wife and son ran away. He was never able to find them. This dented his spirit even more.

Through all the years, I made a conscious effort to be with him, to share in his life, to filter through all his pain and loneliness and try to understand him.

After Dad died, alcohol controlled Claude's life. However, he was able to work and care for this woman and her children. He was a master car-builder and

Uncurling Freedom

restorer, a trade he learned at the reform school in Kenya.

Anthony joined the British Army and was posted to Germany where he was involved in drugs. For the next 20 years, drugs mangled his life. He was dishonorably discharged from the Army.

Claude Louis helped Anthony through his drug befuddled life. He pulled him from gutters, helped with rehab, took him into his home — over and over again. We even paid for a rehab center to help him. He managed to complete the course and moved away from drugs. However his mind and character were warped.

The woman finally left Claude Louis, and he was down to bare bones again. The British Social Services provided a small flat and medical services, along with a vehicle. Other than these tangible things, there was nothing to live for. He continued his life of drinking, smoking and drugs, all alone in that little flat.

I was able to connect my sisters to Claude and Anthony. Initially they did not want anything to do with their brothers. Money had been stolen during a visit,

Uncurling Freedom

and they thought their brothers took it. It turned out other people were the thieves.

Claude and Anthony were shifty and untrustworthy, because they had nothing as children. They were enticed by the "things" of others. The reform school did not reform them.

Claude Louis loved me so much. Each time I travelled through the UK to and from Kenya, I stopped to share some love with him. He waited for those times, and once again I saw the same smile the angels witnessed at his birth. Then it would be gone again, because I was gone.

In May 2007, just before our planned furlough, my sisters called and said, "Please come as soon as possible. Claude Louis is in the hospital and very ill with lung cancer and mesothelioma."

I changed my ticket and we all arrived at his bedside. He lay in the bed, connected to all kinds of machines. When he saw my face, he said, "Lorna, you have come and you are wearing the watch I gave you." To hear him say this from his death bed rendered me unable to move with sorrow. He loved me.

Uncurling Freedom

Pleasure and light surrounded his smile. When I touched his wilting body, such regret permeated through me. I was immediately thrown back to our childhood, questioning my choices and the direction in life I took.

Betty said, "Thank you for coming. Claude Louis waited until he could see you again, hug you and touch your face."

He died on the eighth day of May. All his siblings, together for the first time in decades, stood around his bed. His face was more beautiful in death that it had been in life. He was finally at rest. For Claude Louise, all the pain was erased. But we four still had to live within our steel cages.

Before his death he pleaded, "Lorna, please take my ashes back home to Seychelles where Mum was born and is buried."

My sisters kept the ashes of this beautiful boy, and in August of 2009, I was able to take him home.

Mum's family did not want her buried in the family plot, but my cousin Bernard was able to allow her burial there. When it came time for Claude Louis'

Uncurling Freedom

ashes to be buried, the family refused. Eventually I sprinkled them in the sea and the graveyard. He was home.

Even though I am a Christian, I asked, "Why God was this amazingly beautiful brother of mine put through such a horrific life, with no open door to walk to freedom. What did Claude Louis do wrong? Why did Christians at the church in Nairobi deal deathly attacks and blows to a cripple already crushed by colonial bias and color? These were the ones who should not see color, but a lost soul. Their actions sent him away."

Some Christians act like invisible assassins.

I look into a pool of water and what do I see looking back at me? This person who is aged and in massive pain, because I was not there for this beautiful boy, my brother Claude Louis. Was I like a con-joined twin, focused only on my own beauty and safety, prepared to have the other twin removed and even die, just so I could survive? Perhaps I did this to him.

"You have him back God, and once again the angels are smiling. They see the beautiful face and spirit you gave him. You allowed him to pass through

Uncurling Freedom

such black waters. I weep as I write these things. The agony and pain never diminish, but I know one day we shall see each other's faces."

I think of my beloved brother and continue to write, "I do know that inside you, Claude Louis, you never really turned away from the God who offered you salvation. It was buried beneath all life's inflicted pain on your soul. It was hidden behind the agony of your life. I saw glimpses of it when our faces touched each other.

"You survived enormous struggles. Your hopes and dreams were mere illusions. You lived to work, and in work found some form of solace as you re-created and restored cars. You feared being left alone when Dad died. The chasm of emptiness faced you and the world out there was too dangerous. A beautiful boy, you disarmed me with your guilelessness. But at the same time, you could take advantage of me.

"You were torn away from your land of Kenya and lived in a foreign land. At least now all those years of torture have ended. You will see Mum and Dad again. You rest under the shadow of your God."

Uncurling Freedom

Uncurling Freedom

WHERE IS HOME?

After four-and-a half decades in Africa, we finally arrived back in the USA with two suitcases each. We gave all we had to serve God.

The moment my foot touched US soil, I wanted to turn around, step back on the plane and head home. To touch down on African soil, bend to kiss it, and inhale the pungent rain. Such an exhilarating difference! I felt the loss of leaving my people and land behind, while this huge gulf of emptiness faced me. There was nothing in the US to connect me.

Living in the US was like being in a square, all sanitized and predictable. Few challenges. No real danger, excitement or fear. This land was not the real

Uncurling Freedom

world. In Africa I stepped outside that square into the limitless horizon, where the earth and sky met. Incredible pain throbbed in my chest when I was not in Africa. In the US, I just wandered around.

The most painful part was the church we had been associated with for over 25 years. They hardly knew we were here. At its mission conference, the "notables" held the floor, while we sat in the pew wondering why we felt so alone.

I was challenged by God to celebrate everything I have in this foreign land: a Savior, life, family, grandchildren, siblings, a roof over my head, a car. Here I have food, financial supply, a few good friends, and the memories of living an amazing life in Kenya, Rwanda, Sudan, and Ukraine.

People actually do believe in me. Basically, I enjoy good health. I am conscious of the positive and do not focus or feed my soul on what I do not have — my Africa.

Africans owned resilience, patience and hope (kufumulia) through hardship and war. They were an example to me to keep pressing on. To never give up

Uncurling Freedom

hope. The brilliant white toothy smile of a stranger I passed on the street, the ready greeting and handshake of that stranger. The welcome and encompassing into their lives brought me close to their hearts, to feel safe and wanted. They journeyed step by step (hatua kwa hatua) into each day, confronted by all its challenges.

The pain of Africa haunts me when I am away from it. When I smell its soil again, my heart and soul connect to that loss, come alive. I feel home again.

Now I feel lost and wondering. The need of so many hungry Africans is almost like an addiction I must serve. Perhaps this satiates my own need to be cherished. If I help others in some strange way, I am helping myself.

My heart beats like an African drum. It makes me yearn for African skies, sounds, faces, and smells. I am certain Africa is part of me, until death do us part. No matter how far apart we are, I belong there. My heart belongs to Africa.

I cannot really describe Africa without talking about the animals, the beautiful sunsets and sunrises,

Uncurling Freedom

the lush green landscape during the rainy seasons, the sweeping savannas, and the pure gorgeousness of it all.

And the people: Africa has the friendliest people, always with smiles to greet you and a kind word. Yes, there are parts of Africa that are dangerous. And Africa has its share of slums.

But when I'm in Africa, I'm happy. When I return to the west, I become depressed and homesick. I feel Africa. It's a life-changing place to visit. It changed me for the better.

Africa is where I need to be at my days' end. "Please God, let me go home to Africa."

Uncurling Freedom

JOURNEY OF FAITH

I was born a Roman Catholic, with a devout father who was passionate about God. He left my life when I was 13, but the deposit of faith he put in me was one thing that drew me to God. It was not something tangible I could hold on to or even explain. It was just there as an example and a legacy from him.

I was very unhappy with my Roman Catholic faith. I balked at having to do penance and make confessions, asking a priest to stand in God's place and forgive me. I even made up sins, just to see what the priest would do or say. He was unmoved, and just gave me reams of rosary beads to recite. I knew there had to be more, but how could I find that something more?

Uncurling Freedom

When I attended elementary school in Kenya, I met a missionary's daughter who we all thought was too spiritual. When we went to high school, she was the only one I knew at the new school. We teamed up and I started visiting her home and church. An American former wire tapper called Jim Voss visited our church, and when the call for salvation was made, I ran to the front. My turbulent journey of faith had started, and it was uphill all the way. Surviving life itself took all my energy, but to stay saved and continue required even more.

Throughout my life, God dropped vital people close to me. They held my hands up, encouraged me and kept me walking. The missionaries in Kenya who started me on my journey were very wise. They had no expectations for how I should measure up. They simply started me on my journey, wisely stood back and allowed God to do all the work. He has done so in spite of all the personal attacks and challenges.

"Victorious living doesn't mean a life free from problems. Victorious living means overcoming each

Uncurling Freedom

problem." - Cecil Murphey, "Knowing God, Knowing Myself"

Diani writes, "Do not look at those who hurt you, Mum. Look into my eyes and see the love that is there for YOU. You have been spoken to by mere men whose words have shattered your dreams. They commanded you to fly again, but you were unable to. You are just a small sparrow with broken, torn and featherless wings. Mum, the deepest death to self is by suffering. You are waiting in a corner for a healing touch from the Supreme Being. Waiting for him to command you to fly."

As Ester Nicholson says, "Secrets keep us sick. They keep us in shame and uncertainty. Secrecy is the ideal environment for sin to grow until ultimately you're taken captive by thought patterns, deeds, and habits. And staying in darkness intensifies your cycle of secrecy and slavery to sin."

If something matters to me, it matters to God. I see the revelation of His goodness. The fear of the Lord grips my heart because of the severity of His presence. If I do not know Him well, I cannot represent him well.

Uncurling Freedom

I was continually surprised by His goodness and had to learn and accept his blessings. I learned to never apologize for them, however unworthy I felt, no matter who tried to crush and wipe me out.

I need to be a worshipper, because worship reveals my heart. What is really in there? Am I filled with wickedness and depravity or an overpowering touch of God?

Am I a hypocrite when I cease to be compassionate and loving, to withhold the heart of God from a desperate people? So many times on my journey I have been in this position of turmoil, almost as if I were knocked out.

The cross is the single overriding objective. All else bends to His objective in my life. My chains fall off, my heart is free, and I empty myself of all but love. Only the journey is important.

Many times I ended up face down on the grimy earth, hardly able to breathe because of the pain. Then I lifted up my eyes and saw the hills. The process started all over again: shoulders up, head up, body up, slowly standing to start again on the commissioned journey.

Uncurling Freedom

Slowly the breath and flickering flame ignited, and I stood.

I constantly ask, "Lord how long, oh Lord will this go on?" He never says anything about the timing, only that I must set my eyes on the goal and complete the journey.

He knows my endurance levels and wants to notch me up more and more. So I will stand strong. A greater battle arises. I must be ready for it. Grinding my teeth and biting my tongue, I am forced to bless and forgive, to get on with what God wants of my life. May I not be sidetracked by distractions that are self-destructive.

Psalms 119:54, "*Your principles have been the music of my life throughout the years of my pilgrimage.*" (JBP)

This is how I spend my life, obeying your commandments, oh Lord. You are mine! I promise to obey your words.

When I strive for significance, I actually undermine my significance. In reality I am significant

Uncurling Freedom

because I do what He says—obey. God and I are strong as one.

My beloved daughter Diani says, "I love you so much, Mum. I am praying you remain faithful to your heavenly Father, as I have only ever seen you do. You are sacrificially generous to others. Take time to be generous to yourself."

With such affirmation my journey is tolerable.

Life isn't about how to survive the storm, but how to dance in the rain. Anyone who says sunshine brings happiness has never danced in the rain.

Some things I did not take care of in the first mile of my journey, messed me up in the last mile. This assignment necessitates constant drawing from God. It takes courage to see truth and reverse the course of where my life started. I choose courage and emotional exposure over being comfortable. This nourishes my spirit and is leading me into a wholehearted life.

The words in Second Samuel 22 remind me I am caught by his love. He reaches down and pulls me out of the ocean of hate where I am drowning. God sticks by me and surprises me with his love.

Uncurling Freedom

When I placed all the pieces of my life before him, God made my life complete. When I cleaned up my act, he gave me a fresh start. Indeed, I've kept alert to God's ways. I have not taken God for granted. Every day I review the ways he works. I try not to miss a trick. I feel put back together, and I am watching my steps. When I opened the book of my heart to his eyes, God rewrote the text of my life.

"Grace embraces you before you prove anything and after you've done everything wrong." - Ann Voskamp

Throughout my entire life, I have been more disliked for whose I am, than admired for who I am not. I do not seek revenge, but the ability to be a strong forgiver.

I was asked, "Lorna, is it possible to forget all the terrible things that happened to you when you were child?"

"No, but I did learn from them and became a stronger person. The darkness and fragments of my life left me in pain, and I wondered if I would ever be whole."

Uncurling Freedom

Even now, the darkness comes too often, too quickly, and I am unable to fend it off. The fabric of myself is hanging on by worn threads. A survivor, in shattered disposable pieces. I am learning to pick them up, try to reassemble and carry on with life in an extraordinary way. Nothing is ever the same and I have to change tracks.

I often wonder about life ruts. With some broken people, whole fields of ruts lie in their wake. Do they sometimes wonder who they are and where they are going?

In the "Long Walk to Freedom," Nelson Mandela wrote, "To be free is not merely to cast off my chains, but to live in a way that respects and enhances the freedom of others."

Radical obedience in crises leads me to a higher place in the Lord. Then he releases me to demonstrate what he looks like.

As I look outside my window, the trees seem dead. Gone are all the brilliant lavish green leaves. They shade and cover up so much brown. Winter brings dormancy. It is a period in a trees' cycle when growth

Uncurling Freedom

and development are temporarily stopped. This minimizes activity and conserves energy.

As I face this dormant season in my life, it is imperative that I understand this too is a time of preparation. As growth slows, and the vibrancy of many years of service and fruitfulness end, I feel so barren.

Unknown to me, God is allowing a season of rest and rejuvenation, internal strength and growth to transform me. It is a time to develop inner strength of character. This development is vital if I am to keep going and be disciplined to survive the hard times. To be able to hear his passionate voice who says in this dark place that he rejoices over me with singing. He will give me victory. He will renew my life and bring gladness. What a painfully gorgeous picture! He will snatch me up and out of the darkness that engulfs me, and he and I will sing our song together.

Like a dormant tree, when I am tired will I stand firm, even when there is roiling inside? Will I allow the storage of inner strength to eventually

Uncurling Freedom

bloom? Can I daily take up my cross and follow Christ? None of this is exciting. Much of the time it is boring.

God does have amazing things in store for me. He wants me to be fulfilled and blossom into a beautiful flower. As His light shines into the darkness of my dormancy, suddenly I will see what actually is in my heart.

This restructuring is needed to complete the journey and be prepared for what he has next for me.

Uncurling Freedom

VIGILANT PROTECTION

Problems never leave me where I started. I face them daily and finally understand how these problems have shaped my life. I am stronger. I am closer to God. I have learned to endure hard times, because of God's grace and protection.

Today, I am strong and able because of the pain, rejection, discouragement, verbal and emotional abuse, and all of life's experiences — whether glorious, mundane or fearful. I hope my journey will help others see how God took me, an insignificant individual from the Dark Continent, and completely changed my life. Then through me, he affected the lives of children. God trusted me to be his Image-Bearer, to love the people of my land of Kenya, and to share his redemption story.

Uncurling Freedom

His vigilant care has kept me from danger, prostitution and possible rape in Kenya and South Africa. These challenges were expected of me, a person of questionable pedigree.

My biggest challenge was to keep my mouth shut. Having endured verbal and emotional abuse, this was the most difficult of all lessons. I wanted to volley back in kind what was shouted to me. Agape taught me how to continuously bless and forgive.

Words I speak can never be taken back. The quality and damage I meter out in using them must be measured in order that I do not annihilate another person. Christ spoke redemptive words, and as a believer I should follow that pattern. When I am attacked verbally or emotionally, how I respond to that attack shows if my flesh is still alive or dead. If alive, then I will react. If dead, then the Holy Spirit in me will enable me to have a meek and quiet spirit

Agape is self-sacrificial love revealed and esteemed in God's acts of thoughtfulness, extravagant generosity, vigilant protection, and tender restoration of

Uncurling Freedom

shattered lives. He attributes value and changes us from glory to glory.

As a believer, my reaching out should offer this value at all times. The person I am today is due to the birthing process and the learning of life's lessons. I travel within the spiritual birth canal. It is only here that I am ever able to see and assimilate the pain of others, understand rejection, discouragement and abuse. It is because of these inner dealings of God in my life, that I reflect His glory in and through the lives of others I touch.

Am I to allow a satanic seed to be planted in me to demean and attack others like a predator or parasite? An example is a picture of the Hutu tribe in Rwanda verbally attacking the Tutsi tribe on countrywide radio broadcasts, reducing them to metaphorical cockroaches. The tragic result of such words ended in the slaughter of over 800,000 people in 100 days.

Isaiah wrote, *"For the breath of the ruthless is like a rain storm against the wall"* (Isaiah 25:4 JBP).

When I demean another person, it misuses and enlarges weakness in that person. The verbal devaluing

Uncurling Freedom

capitalizes on half-truths, as in: "She is a controlling person." "He is greedy." "They are gossips."
The momentum of this action then snowballs as I engage in helping others to see and share in an opinion about the offender. It eventually destroys the individual.

Demeaning others is Satan's nature working through me. This practice is strongly condemned by Jesus, *"I say to you that everyone who is angry with his brother shall be guilty before the court: and whoever says to his brother 'You good-for-nothing,' shall be guilty before the Supreme Court; and whoever says, 'You fool,' shall be guilty enough to go into the fiery hell"* (Matthew 5:22 JBP).

Agape covers and graciously protects my value and his imprint in my flawed nature. It offers me the needed redemptive environment of safety where I am given an open door to repent. This allows for God's transformation of my life and character. The door is open, but I can choose whether or not to enter it.

When I demean others, it is a potent and transmittable action void of conscience and has mutual retribution tactics. My very sin nature is to demean

Uncurling Freedom

others. Worse still, when I am demeaned, I measure out that portion to others. Those who dislike me project their actions and motives on me.

The Agape of God carries no distinction or level of approval. His love accepts drunks, prostitutes, killers, a fellow trusted worker, a minister in my church who spurns me, anyone who seeks to stamp out the light of God in my heart. Agape deals with all of these without being two-faced. It is a sign I am truly being conformed into the image of Christ.

This change of behavior seems to be an impossible feat. I have been given the open door in taking him into myself. This transforms me from a beast into a true daughter of God. I am a bond slave of Jesus, and part of that process is for God to help himself to my life. Is he going to help himself to me or am I taken up with my conception of what and who I am going to be?

Uncurling Freedom

Uncurling Freedom

EMOTIONAL COLOR

The palette of my emotional color falls into the green and purple ranges.

Purple reflects spiritual wisdom, mystery, creativity, independence, shame, melancholy and loneliness. It combines the stability of blue and the energy of red. Purple is associated with royalty and symbolizes power, nobility, luxury and ambition.

Green reflects growth, hope, passion, jubilation, exhilaration and peace.

These colors have emerged from the original black tones of my childhood. I witness them in the following beautiful portrait. Other rainbow colors flit in and out of my palette.

Uncurling Freedom

FAERIE GOD MOTHER

Gentle, beauty woman,

With speedy tongue and mind,

Pain buried deep,

But slowly, unlocked—for me, for all of us.

Beautiful woman, who chastises gently,

With words of pure love,

Not myself to be chastised,

Not my heart to be trodden

But my own pain

My own loathing to be chastised—oh so softly.

Loving woman, with the depth

Of life, lived, with pain

Slowly unlocked—for me for all of us.

Giving woman, with all her heart,

In all honesty, earnestness,

Deep-rooted faith.

Uncurling Freedom

Deeper than the pain could ever go,
Roots that speak to God, regardless
Depths that no one will know
Or appreciate.

My faerie godmother,
Who gives me things?
But better always,
Gives me the love,
The love I need, the example to follow.

Gentle, honest woman,
Who should have danced,
To our astonishment,
But instead
Has wings to fly her,
Into her farthest dreams,
Into her very God.

With all my love and thanks, Nom

Uncurling Freedom

Uncurling Freedom

HEART TRAUMA

We lived in three thatched-roofed rooms in Thika, Kenya. Our front yard reached beyond the horizon. Philo, Elior and Diani took safaris into the coffee plantations and birds of paradise flower fields.

Shattering that idyllic place on January 9, 1979, Zack developed recurring left-arm pains and shortness of breath. I counted the diminishing beats on his wrist with alarm.

Running off into the bush in bare feet with thorns and grass cutting my legs and feet, I banged on the door of my neighbor. I pleaded with Moree to care for our children while I took Zack to Nairobi Hospital, thirty miles away.

I was able to get Zack into our beat-up Peugeot station wagon. The exhaust pipe dangled in the mud as

Uncurling Freedom

we barreled down the drive. Elior ran after the car shouting, "Please don't die, Dad."

At Nairobi Hospital, Zack was hurried from the emergency room into the ICU. While I waited, the money question blitzed through my mind. We lived on so little and had no medical coverage.

When the doctor finally appeared, he said, "Your husband has a 50-50 possibility of survival." He explained the massive damage to his lower heart area. Thus began ten days of tests, trips by ambulance to various hospitals in Nairobi, with Zack hooked up to machines in the ICU.

Missionaries, Kenyan pastors, and supporters joined in prayer.

On the tenth day, a cardiologist entered Zack's room and said, "Stop limping about. Get out of here, walk and live. There is no evidence of heart damage."

All evidence of a destroyed heart was gone.

When I went to pay the hospital bill, the cashier handed me back half the amount I paid and said, "Someone has paid the rest."

Uncurling Freedom

We left the hospital with cash in hand and a healed heart. Since then, Zack has never had trouble with his heart.

Uncurling Freedom

Uncurling Freedom

WHAT'S MY STORY?

My story revolves around my strong swimmer's heart.

Mum was such a beauty. When she walked down the street in Dar-es-salaam, Tanzania (Tanganyika), people stopped to look at her. They thought she was a film star.

It was from her womb that I made my entry into the world. Through the birth canal, swimming up to light and air — in time to discover God knew my name. From the inner depths of Mum's body, God called me up.

My journey began below the ocean's surface. That calm but continually still turquoise, mysterious and majestic expanse. Free from gravity and filled with

Uncurling Freedom

gold light. Flecked and twisting with sea creatures. My life's challenge was to get to the surface.

I swam through deep royal blue waving carpets, spread in a rainbow spectrum. Magical waves of coral, lavender and turquoise enveloped my body. At times it was radiantly crystal clear. When a storm blew, desolate darkness descended in the swelling angry and unforgiving ocean.

I wanted to make it to that shore and horizon. Having all this majesty surrounding me, why would I want to get to the surface?

Swimming from the birth canal up and up through all the murk and mire, the dazzling ocean's brilliance was a challenging decision. It proved more arduous than I anticipated. Someone was always bent on poking me back down.

Swimming gave me an amazingly gold strong heart. It helped me leave behind in the depths all the violence of racism, marital discord and abuse. These I bled, fought, loved too much for.

Uncurling Freedom

How did I make it through? I longed to reach out from the depths and clutch hands as they rescued me and pulled me up.

Zack, along with many others, poked me back down.

As a strong swimmer, each time I was shoved down, I struggled back up for air, then down again and back up.

People shouted from the shore and told Zack to stop. They rode out in small boats and yelled at him, only to be met by his blocked ears and a deaf heart. He was determined to keep me in my place — down. The thought of my strength, light, beauty and ability threatened him.

Others who knew the real me, were in the water alongside me, pushing me up and up and up. A shoulder to stand on, a hand reaching out to tug me up. Never alone.

Due to childhood abuse, the scene was set. My automatic response was to accept abuse, to be silent and non-confrontational. Bullies hoodwinked me into

Uncurling Freedom

silence then and now. Within my marriage, an arrogant, proud, stubborn and illiterate man was in control.

So many times I questioned, what attracted me to him? He was handsome, captivating, and friendly to everyone around him. What lurked beneath that glistening exterior was unimaginable and unseen. What lived in his ocean's depths?

Stroke after stroke, I ploughed my way to the surface. It was close. My fingers reached out. So many times, emotional anchors attached to my feet forced me down.

The ability to keep swimming has streamlined my faith. All my adversity and pain, whether good or bad, was honed and chiseled away. Those unnecessary things that needed removing allowed me to see myself for who I truly am — beautiful beyond depiction. I see myself as God made me from Mum's womb. I am learning my own name.

"Out of suffering have emerged the strongest souls, the most massive characters are seared with scars." - Khalil Gibran

Uncurling Freedom

Second Peter 1 reminds me I have been given everything necessary to live a godly life.

This truth includes the understanding of God's great redemptive gift, self-control, endurance, devotion, knowledge and kindness. If I forget God's grace, it will breed un-forgiven living in me.

These are the qualities that dot my life. I seek to live by them with more understanding and commitment. My mind is slowly being set free from mental and emotional bondage. These torments warped and twisted the real me, by continual attacks and conflicts. I believed the captivating lies which spiraled into depression, fear, constant suicide addiction, low self worth and condemnation.

The strengths and lessons learned in the dark depths enable me to finally walk on dry land. Currently, I still struggle to make it to the surface. One day that final stroke up and out of the water will take place, like a whale pounding and thrashing into the sky. When this occurs, I will be on solid ground — walking, leaping and free.

Uncurling Freedom

Swimming is still a central part of my life. Now I stay on top of the water. As I look into the depths, they rarely have any power to draw me back down.

When my body touches the water, there is instant healing. Wherever I am, I find a pool. Whether riding from the African bush of Kitui in a petrol tanker or walking several miles in Rwanda. As my body enters the water, I detox and debrief to face life's challenges anew.

No more a prisoner.

Uncurling Freedom

REMEMBERING MUM
(*Se souvenir de maman, Fr*)

Set into a wrinkled face, her bright shining blue eyes followed my every move. Her soft wrinkled and bent fingers, reached out to my whole life. I should have stopped at her carefully tended little home for a cup of tea. Or I should have called her on the phone. But my friends came first. Would any of them have done what she did for me?

When she called me on the phone, I was always in a hurry. I cut her off and rushed to do things for others. All she wanted was a touch of my love in her ear or to brush her hand on mine.

I was angry with her and frowned into that loving face when all she wanted to do was guide me

Uncurling Freedom

through paths of life she had experienced, to save me from myself. I was too proud and arrogant.

She was marvelous. She loved me. She sacrificed her whole life, so I could be what to her was only a mirage. She helped my dreams become reality. The price was never too great in her generous sacrificial living.

My childhood in Kenya was filled with expeditions. We camped on Lake Navisha and heard hippos take their midnight walks. We climbed snow-capped Mount Kenya and swam in the warm and shimmering Indian Ocean. Mum made sure we partook, smelled and touched all that was brutal, filthy, and demeaning in the largest slum in Africa, then all that was stunningly indescribable. Journeys most children only fantasize about.

From my childhood through school and college and eventually marriage, she was always by my side. Perhaps not physically, because at times, continents separated us, but in every other way. When I needed help with my little ones, she was there for me. She

Uncurling Freedom

cleaned baby bottles, lining them up sparkling clean at the sink. Easy for me to grab and go.

A few years ago, we buried this wonderful woman. I returned home to find this poem she left for me from an anonymous author:

THE TIME IS NOW

If you are ever going to love,
Love me now while I can know
The sweet and tender feelings
Which from true affection flow.

Love me now while I am living
Do not wait until I'm gone
And then have it chiseled in marble
Sweet words on ice-cold stone.

If you have tender thoughts of me
Please let me know now.
If you wait until I'm sleeping

Uncurling Freedom

There will be death between us
And I will not hear you then.

So if you love me, even a little bit
Let me know while I am living
So that I can treasure it.

Now she is gone and I am sick with guilt. I never told her what she meant to me. Worse, I did not treat her as she deserved to be treated. I was too critical, too short-tempered and too stingy with praise. She gave her unconditional love, but I saw that love as if it tainted those around me.

The world is filled with sons, daughters and children like me. We shun our parents, sending them off to state facilities. We do not care for them in old age as they cared for us as children. By honoring our parents, God notices and rewards us with the blessings of a long life. Could we not learn from Africa, where old people are treasured, admired, respected and revered?

Uncurling Freedom

It is not too late to teach my children to honor the parents who still live. By honoring the physical beings, they honor God.

I watched young children in the Sudan who approached parents and grandparents with heads bowed. They extended a hand of blessing by laying it on the bowed head. The child walked away, smiling.

When I think of the times I cut Mum off, I feel ashamed. I retorted back to her. I glared at her in anger when all she wanted was to share truth and guidance. I could have included her in a trip out and did not. It would take too much time for her to get ready.

My children loved her. She was there at the birth of six of her granddaughters. They often turned to her for comfort and advice. She understood them and cradled them in her heart.

I still search for this Pearl in each room of my home. There is only silence. She is gone. The piano sits silent by the open window where her fingers once graced the keys. She played and sang her favorite French love song.

Uncurling Freedom

Mum died alone, far from all of us on the same exotic Seychelles Islands of her birth, attended to by merciful Catholic sisters.

This beautiful Mum, whose heart I slept and grew beneath for nine months — I miss terribly. Too late she became a person of worth to me, a bittersweet realization. She ignited a fire in my heart and I am who I am today because of her.

Good bye, my beloved Mum. Au revoir ma maman bien-aimée, Fr.

Uncurling Freedom

BIBLICAL MANDATE

While driving around Nairobi collecting medical cargo for Akot Medical Mission, my driver Peter and I saw a man lying on the ground. Outside the church gates, he writhed and shook all over. We drove away and left him lying there, people standing around staring at him. We continued the journey, but my heart was constricted with conviction.

We collected the cargo and headed back up the same road. He still lay foaming at the mouth and shaking uncontrollably. The people continued to watch him behind the church's locked gates and metal barriers.

"Peter, can you please pull over? We cannot just drive by and allow the man to die on the road." This

Uncurling Freedom

was the first time in my life that the practical application of the Samaritan story zoomed into my face. Would I drive away? Would I close my eyes? Would I act high and mighty? Or would I obey and offer help?

I tried to commandeer the bystanders and some of the church people hiding behind locked gates. "Pick this man up," I said, "and move him out of the driveway. How come you just stand here and watch? Have you forgotten the commands of our Lord?" My advantage was I could speak to them in their language.

No response. Only glares.

One young man called Bernard answered my call for help. He unlocked the church gates and the three of us moved the sick man out of harm's way.

I asked Bernard, "Why do people behave like this, especially outside a church?"

"The leader in this church said the Africans do this all the time. This is not the first time. This man is playing sick to get money."

"Are we not commanded to reach out 'to such as these?'"

Bernard hung his head in silence.

Uncurling Freedom

I wiped the man's face with his soiled jacket and removed the foam covering his face from his epileptic fit. Now was the time to put into practice what I read and talked about. This man was not faking it. I laid my hands on him and prayed as the crowd continued to look on.

I said to Peter, "Do you know anyone else who could take this man to a clinic for treatment?" Thankfully, within minutes Peter's friend arrived.

Gratefully, I had the ability to pay for his treatment, and off they went.

The driver took the young man to the clinic. After treatment and supplies of medication and food, he was returned to his little shack in the slums.

As the scene played out that day, God's Word spoke to my spirit. With each event falling into place, "As it is written." God provided a way to help the man with a friend of a friend.

Uncurling Freedom

Uncurling Freedom

DUPLICITOUS CHARACTER

At five feet ten inches, Zack looked like Elvis Presley. He had strong arms and a muscular body from outdoor work as an expert carpenter, builder and designer. Coming from a sheep-rearing country, he had a shallow personality but showed interest in people. Because he was so personable and welcoming, he stood out. He was always seeking attention and affirmation, portraying his expertise in everything. When entering a room, he sucked up all the air, wanting the conversation centered on him.

His face was creased from frowning, with a mouth that sloped down when anyone disagreed with him. He had ADHD and was a slow learner. His controlling method was to say, "If it's worth doing, it's

Uncurling Freedom

worth doing well." Emotionally insecure, he was not able to express his feelings. Because he put up smoke screens, people never knew the "real" Zack.

He loved his tools and making things was his passion — especially creating things for other people and to serve God. His anger, arrogance, emotional and verbal intimidation were used to impress people with his "superior" knowledge. A man so self-obsessed with his own perception of perfection, he made life hell for those around him as he constantly pointed out faults and treated them miserably.

"When you are whole and consistent, there is only one you. You bring that same you wherever you are, regardless of the circumstances. You don't leave parts of yourself behind. You don't have a 'work you,' a 'family you,' and a 'social you.' You are YOU all the time." Global Leadership by So-young Kang, Catalyst & CEO of the Awaken Group.

People do not expect the abuser to lie about who he is. He does so continually, as if this is normal.

This truth described Zack's reality. It was hard to recognize him because of his inauthentic face mask.

Uncurling Freedom

He knew exactly how to target people who were easy to manipulate and deemed weak. He appeared benevolent, so it never struck others that they may be seeing a warped view of him. How could it be possible, that such a charming man could lie and pretend so expertly?

On the mission field, we could do nothing about this situation. We just had to keep going. If we sought counsel or help, it would mean being pulled away from our beloved Africa.

This man, who acted like a boy, took power away from me by slowly and steadily denigrating my self-esteem. His methods were harmful and clever, as he never made the covert abuse obvious. It was invisible, pre-meditated and intentional. When used systematically, it affected my physiological well-being. I questioned my perception of reality and grew intensely insecure.

Identity and self-esteem are closely related. Developing healthy self-esteem and a strong sense of identity affects our mental health, behaviors and how we relate to people.

Uncurling Freedom

This harsh man attacked me without empathy. He was so involved with his own concerns, he did not consider what other people felt. He made himself appear bigger by forcing people to buckle under him. Diminishing empathy produced increased pain for the abused — for me.

I was regularly crushed into submission. Small drips of love escaped from me, which I then poured into other wounded hearts and lives. I had the ability to see their pain, because it was mirrored in my own.

Zack's behavior was reinforced by the deafening shame of my silence and the enormity of my failure not to hold him accountable. I was scared spitless. So were others around him. He never missed the opportunity to flay me or to gloat when someone else dressed me down. He watched, smiled and nodded his head.

Then he would ask the spiritual question, "Why does she not submit to me?"

With my marriage partner, my hope was that our hearts would beat as one, resonating to the same melody. We would thrive on mutuality, reciprocity and

Uncurling Freedom

the freedom to challenge one another's behaviors without fear. But our marriage was disharmonic. We were "off key" — resulting in lifelong crashing cymbals, conflict, hostility, disunity and opposition. My notes were sharp. His were flat. No other composition was available to bring the pieces of life together. No crescendo and no sweet melodies.

Once when I challenged Zack, I said, "We need to start packing up the house and storing our things for furlough."

Because I told him what we needed to do, he left the house for three days. I had no idea where he was. Those were the days with no mobile phones.

Where fear reigned, no intimacy, trust, companionship or balm existed. Broken trust seriously damaged our marriage. Worse, no evidence existed of repentance or the desire for a changed heart. He was never wrong. I was never right.

I felt like a snail, carefully navigating life, sensitive to the slightest discord of sound or movement, pulling myself back into my hard exterior for

Uncurling Freedom

protection. This caused me to distance myself from people in general.

Zack used jokes at my expense. For example, he once said, "I remember our wedding like it was yesterday — remember what a rotten day yesterday was."

Using my hurt as an excuse to hurt me more, he kept making the same jokes, no matter how I felt or what I said. I was treated like an idiot. Instead of my thoughts and ideas having the same weight as his, he would say, "This is the right and only way to do this."

He did this to "train" me how to behave and speak in a certain way. I had to watch when his finger crossed his lips, his signal for "Be silent, and do not speak." I might receive a hefty kick under the table or a deep frown of his reproof.

This was how he trained our dogs. Down dog. Chastisement does not ever belong in a relationship.

Love bombing made me forget anything was ever wrong as he would do something so overwhelmingly gracious. His kindness, loving and selflessness, would sweep me off my feet into insensibility and amnesia. Such heartfelt delight so easily offered was obliterated when the devilish face appeared.

After this love bombing, the expectation always, was sex. I could not submit myself to such treachery. I was repelled. This enraged Zack, and his violent behavior increased. The darkness of this malignant person was terrifying. The lengths he would go to bring me down and destroy me were unspeakable.

This roller coaster was the most dangerous part of emotional abuse, because it acted as an eraser for all the terror he put me through. It was used to confuse the resentment and pain I developed in response to his abuse. It was almost impossible to disengage or to instantly forget what happened. This treatment eventually caused brain changes and mental illness. I was continually walking on multi-layers of eggs shells, almost as if I owned a hatchery.

Children who grow up with this type of malignant toxic person have no frame of reference to what is normal. Some become similar perpetrators. No matter how often they promise things will be different,

Uncurling Freedom

abusers do not change. At some level, they know what they are doing is wrong, but they do not care.

As I learned the ways abuse happened, it was the first step to emotionally arming myself. To recognize the abuse for what it was and begin to move on.

Slowly the real Zack emerged, but I kept hoping and praying he would see what he was inflicting on his family — that he would grieve and repent. How could he gain the benefit of a good marriage when he stubbornly continued his behavior? No repentance, no reconciliation.

What would bring me joy and release? How could I break the bonds that tied me in knots for decades?

Before, when looking in the mirror, I saw this ugly, unhappy, wrinkled woman. She was worn down, twisted and shunned by abuse. When I realized God's hand permanently rested on my shoulders, I began to look in the mirror and say, "Lord, look at what your love has done."

It changed my entire perspective.

CHANGE: MABADILIKO (KISWAHILI)

After several months of preparation, the day arrived. Zack would depart for New Zealand to seek medical assistance. On Thursday, March 8, Zack said he was fasting for three days. I had no idea why.

Friday, March 9: "Why are you fasting, Zack?"

"Because there is no change in you, Lorna. I am waiting for you to change. If you do not change, then I am out of here. I do not want you going to the airport when Philo takes me. We live in a hypocritical marriage."

Shock covered me like a cold blanket. Blame and shame laid on me. I was the guilty one yet again. Countless thoughts assailed my mind.

The end of an era — a marriage — a life divested of everything that had meaning. A life spent

Uncurling Freedom

serving God in Africa, in the USA, in Ukraine. I felt a sense of relief. This was the first time he saw the reality of the situation, yet he would go his own way. But emotionally, I saw all I had given to this life, this marriage. Now, it would end in hopelessness. We would each go away bruised and tormented, broken and alone.

March 10: In my rage and fury, I walked across parking lots, kicking stones, tarmac, digging grass out with my shoes. With my fists clenched in my shorts pockets, God's incredible words dropped into my heart.

"Would you allow Zack to go to New Zealand without hope? Could you offer him an olive branch?"

Steaming, I walked back to the car, and asked Zack those same questions. So began a healing moment, 24 hours before Zack left for New Zealand.

Words gushed out of me. "We have damaged each other all these years. We took care of others as the Lord lived through us. We gave our all to others but we never gave to one another."

In retrospect, my silence through the years had done more damage that I could have imagined. I

Uncurling Freedom

reached crossroads so many times within my marriage. But God's hand rested on my shoulder, guiding me.

Such weeping and wailing on that day, words could hardly be uttered. Deep groans barely escaped our throats. Feeling so betrayed and besieged. At the time of our own need, we found ourselves abandoned and adrift. Our hearts broke in the freedom of speaking truth, allowing ourselves to actually feel. We might never be able to stop the weeping. Never had I seen Zack bawling his eyes out.

Who could know at the beginning how it would end 52 years later? The entire trauma was suffered by us both. Unless a miracle happened, this marriage was not redeemable. We had walked and lived each day in our emotional dysfunction, somehow unable to disengage ourselves and move on. Two shattered people who God chose to work through in Africa.

This overwhelming and bottomless emptiness seeped into every pore of our being. We were married, yet alone. We were not part of the church community in the US as we were always outside the desirable circle. Who was there to reach out and touch our lives? We

Uncurling Freedom

were unable to help ourselves, and there was scarce empathy.

We had spent our lives reaching out to hurting, needy and devastated people. So much time helping the world that our own feelings of indiscernible emptiness and loss were packed down tight and hard. We functioned on the outside, but inside were empty shells. Why could we not reach out for one another?

In spite of all the trauma, we actually lived together and developed the courage to continue. But with no one to uphold us and bring us near, to caress us with soothing hands of compassion. My life was described as a shell with no love, cherishing, respect, or value for my uniqueness, no house, gems or clothes. No home. I just wanted to be held, folded close and nurtured.

We gave all to everyone else who had so little. But to each other, we gave nothing. We had come almost to life's end, and did not even have one another. He left for New Zealand with just two duffle bags.

Uncurling Freedom

In spite of such loss, I kept marching on. But after Zack left, the cost brought me to a physical and emotional breakdown.

Uncurling Freedom

UNCURLED FREEDOM

I am getting better each day. I have changed, but it is not the change Zack demanded. It is the change Christ wants. In offering hope and the olive branch, change signified peace and reconciliation.

But I am not going back to being the person Zack wants me to be. He wants me back as I was. He feels safe with the old me.

This was an epiphany, a healing moment and change for me. Maybe for Zack, too.

What meant something to Zack: his tools, work, his impressing appearance of godliness, continual talking to deflect what was really going on between others and us. How sad that truth could not be heard and life changes made years ago. Evading truth — not

Uncurling Freedom

holding Zack accountable when he brutalized his family with his violent words and actions.

Lucy Njoki, my Kenyan soul mate said, "Mama, success nor failure are final. It is the courage to continue that counts."

The Master Crafter, whose hand has always been on my shoulder, will take up his tools to re-craft and mold the days that lie before us. We cannot rewrite our history, but we *can* start a new chapter.

All I can offer God is shame and brokenness. This mosaic life, created before the beginning of time was tarnished, cluttered and obscured with all the rubbish we each brought to our marriage. God seeks once again to see his beautiful creation and design.

Can we allow ourselves to turn back to the God of our youth?

In Africa our lives were filled with excitement, challenges, the exotic blue Indian Ocean, erupting riverbanks, wild animals, unique tribal people, and danger from man and beast. Our existence now seems mundane.

Uncurling Freedom

God has given us our lives to live out again, but this does not mean Zack is absolved. God will have to deal with him.

Sometimes God takes a long time to act suddenly.

I began to uncurl through the power of music. Music woke my heart from a long hibernation. It woke me from my withdrawing inwards in relationships. A tendril of hope grew toward the light. Only when the music started did that "uhuru" (freedom) inhabit my heart, my soul, my legs and fingers.

Although I have no reprieve, in God's time he makes my life sublime. As he raises me up on his shoulders, we dance as one.

I am free.

Uncurling Freedom

REFERENCES

Elisabeth Kubler-Ross

Cecil Murphey

Brene Brown

Adam McHugh

Deuteronomy 33:25 KJV

Philippians 3:14 KJV

First Samuel 1:28 KJV

Matthew 14:29-30 JBP

Hudson Taylor

James 3:2 JBP

Luke 22 KJV

Psalm 66:5 JBP

Dick Joyce

Judges 6:14 KJV

Ester Nicholson

Psalm 119:54 JBP

Second Samuel 22 KJV

Ann Voskamp

Nelson Mandela

Isaiah 25:4 JBP

Matthew 5:22 JBP

Khalil Gibran

Second Peter 1 KJV

So-Young Kang

ACKNOWLEDGEMENTS

My Dad — Luc Bertie — a godly father who showed me God's face (*Un père pieux qui m'a montré le visage de Dieu) Fr.*

My mother — Hélène Sophie — a gifted musician (*un musician doue) Fr.*

My three children, my eight granddaughters, my two sisters.

Rebecca Thesman, my biblical counselor and writing coach.

Half the proceeds of this book will be donated to my Kenya and Rwandan children — for spiritual and physical sustenance and education.

Uncurling Freedom

ABOUT THE AUTHOR

Lorna Westergreen, a pseudonym, has lived a marathon life as a white African missionary. She was born in Kenya and served 45 years in various African countries. Westergreen survived 44 years of abuse within a 52-year marriage, the Mau Mau rebellion and the after-effects of the Rwandan genocide. She also treated the wounded after the US Embassy bombing in Nairobi in 1998.

After leaving Africa, Westergreen has lived a simple life in various places, depending on the hospitality and generosity of others. She is still in the race as a resilient worshipper, administrator, mother, grandmother and multi-tasker. While she is still in the process of recovering from the abuse, she is depending on the Lover of her soul — Almighty God — to do a healing within.

This memoir is Lorna's first book.

Uncurling Freedom

Made in the USA
San Bernardino, CA
16 January 2019